MAHLER: his life and times

# MAHLER

his life and times

*Edward Seckerson*

MIDAS BOOKS

HIPPOCRENE BOOKS
New York

In the same Illustrated Documentary Series

| | |
|---|---|
| BACH | Tim Dowley |
| BEETHOVEN | Ates Orga |
| CHOPIN | Ates Orga |
| DVORAK | Neil Butterworth |
| ELGAR | Simon Mundy |
| HAYDN | Neil Butterworth |
| MAHLER | Edward Seckerson |
| MENDELSSOHN | Mozelle Moshansky |
| MOZART | Peggy Woodford |
| OFFENBACH | Peter Gammond |
| RACHMANINOFF | Robert Walker |
| PAGANINI | John Sugden |
| SHOSTAKOVICH | Eric Roseberry |
| SCHUBERT | Peggy Woodford |
| SCHUMANN | Tim Dowley |
| TCHAIKOVSKY | Wilson Strutte |
| VERDI | Peter Southwell-Sander |

*To my mother*

First published in UK in 1982 by
MIDAS BOOKS
12 Dene Way, Speldhurst,
Tunbridge Wells, Kent TN3 0NX

© Edward Seckerson 1982

ISBN 0 85936 152 7

First published in USA in 1982 by
HIPPOCRENE BOOKS INC
171 Madison Avenue
New York, NY 10016

ISBN 0 88254 662 7

Typesetting by Style Photosetting Ltd, Tunbridge Wells.
Printed and bound at The Pitman Press, Bath.

# Contents

# Introduction

'We cannot see how any of his music can long survive him', wrote one soured New York critic just a few days after Mahler's death in 1911, and for some time it looked very much as though his seemingly rash prophecy might well prove to be all too accurate. But for a distinguished group of 'devotees' who kept his cause alive during this lengthy period of comparative neglect – conductors like Bruno Walter, Willem Mengelberg, Otto Klemperer and Sir John Barbirolli – the dearth of Mahler performances, whether in the concert hall or on gramophone records, continued well into the 60s.

To some extent Mahler was a paradox among great creative geniuses of the past in that he achieved far-reaching success in two careers: the one before, the other after his death. His conducting career began as a means to an end. The success that he achieved in this capacity at least brought him a proportion of time in which to practise his only true and compulsive vocation: that of composition. What could not be bought, however, was acceptance, and recognition for his music was cruelly slow in coming.

Perhaps the key to Mahler's climatic upsurge in the second half of the 20th century has a sociological origin rooted way back at the beginning of the century. Gradually the tight-lipped conservatism and inhibition that had previously rendered his music unfashionably self-indulgent, had disappeared. Creative artists could more acceptably give vent to their private emotions – in public – as it were. People began regarding the likes of Mahler as a mirror in which they might see reflected their own neuroses and through which they might escape from the harsh realities of an increasingly automated and materialistic society into worlds of fantasy and heightened vision. Space-age advances in the 70s only intensified that need still further, and Mahler simply became adopted as the symbol of a new generation's aspirations and insecurities. His was a modern voice but one that could easily be understood. His music, caught as it was between the 19th and 20th centuries, drew sustenance, on the one hand, from the culmination of a great romantic era and, on the other, from the birth of a totally new language in orchestral colour and tonality, to say nothing of structural freedom. 'The symphony is the world! The symphony must embrace everything!', insisted Mahler during a conversation with Sibelius in the autumn of 1907 as if to predict the immense upheaval that was to take place in symphonic music during the 20th century.

As recently as the late 1950s Bruno Walter expressed uncertainty as to where Mahler really stood in the world of music at that time. Had Walter lived to witness the cult which gathered momentum throughout the 1970s, he would have seen his answer emblazened wherever music so much as stirred: a plethora of sell-out performances in concert halls all over the world; recorded cycles of the symphonies, either completed or underway at the time of writing, from no less than eight international conductors; and the name of Gustav Mahler on the lips of people who may never have set foot in a concert hall in their lives.

'My time will come', Mahler once said. And how prophetic those words turned out to be.

MAHLER: his life and times

Gustav Mahler, aged 6.

# 1. Beginnings

*My creative works and my existence are so closely interwoven that if my life flowed as peacefully as a stream through a meadow I believe I would no longer be able to compose anything.*

From the moment of Gustav Mahler's birth in the tiny Bohemian village of Kalist on the 7th July 1860, the foundations were laid for a life beset by doubts, insecurities, rejections and endless soul-searching – fuel in abundance for his, the most potent and temperamental of musical imaginations.

By 1860, Bohemia and Moravia, then crown lands in the Austro-Hungarian monarchy of Franz Joseph I, housed large colonies of Jews who lived, despite increasing liberalism, amidst the uncertainty of anti-semitic feeling. The Mahlers were one such family. 'I am thrice homeless,' Gustav once said, 'as a native of Bohemia in Austria, as an Austrian among Germans, and as a Jew throughout all the world. Everywhere an intruder, never welcomed'.

He was the second, but first surviving, child born to Bernard and

Mahler's birthplace in the village of Kalist, Bohemia.

11

*Left* Marie Mahler, Mahler's mother.
*Right* Bernhard Mahler, Mahler's father.

Marie Mahler. Bernard Mahler, originally a carter or peddler, later rising to the respectable heights of the Jewish *petit bourgeois* by virtue of running his own distillery and off-licence, married Marie, the 20 year old daughter of a soap-maker, in 1857. Her parents saw the marriage as something of an ideal match, when in actual fact nothing could have been further from the truth. Marie married very much against her will. She was in love with someone else and could foresee the hopelessness of what lay ahead.

It was a pitifully loveless marriage, but one which produced no less than fourteen children. Only seven survived infancy: apart from Gustav there were Ernst (b.1861), Leopoldine (b.1863), Alois (b.1867), Justine (b.1868), Otto (b. 1873), and Emma (b. 1875). Tragically, Ernst was to die from the heart disease, hydrocardia, at the age of only thirteen leaving his elder brother isolated and lonely. Ernst was both friend and confidant to Gustav. With him went any semblance of loving companionship in an otherwise unhappy childhood.

At the age of five, when asked what he wanted to be when he grew up, Gustav replied: 'a martyr'. Already his ambition was well on the way to fulfilment. Here he was caught between the

12

antagonisms of his ill-matched parents: a typically 19th century father whose every word was law — coarse, aggressive, tyrannical, ambitious; and his frail mother, lame from birth, to whom he gave out all his love, but whose perpetual suffering and drudgery from one pregnancy to another forever tormented him. The smell of death was always close at hand. Suffering, it seemed, was a matter of course, a way of life.

Mahler's wife, Alma, later wrote that he dreamed his way through childhood. Sure enough it was this self-induced dream-world which was to shelter him from the adversity of his surroundings and very soon supply the fuel for his musical inspirations. Music provided both a retreat and an outlet. All manner of observation from as far back as he could remember was assimilated and later drawn upon, and if we find in his work an extraordinary juxtaposition of tragedy and humour, of the sublime and the ridiculous, it is because this was precisely how those earliest recollections struck him. One notable incident, always considered of great significance in this respect, emerged during Mahler's visit to Sigmund Freud, the famous psychoanalyst, in 1910 — one year before he died. Freud related the episode later in a letter:

'His father, apparently a brutal person, treated his wife very badly, and when Mahler was a young boy there was a specially painful scene between them. It became unbearable to the boy, who rushed away from the house. At that moment, however, a hurdy-gurdy in the street was grinding out the popular Viennese air "O, du lieber Augustin". In Mahler's opinion, the conjunction of high tragedy and light amusement was from there on inextricably fixed in his mind, and the one mood inevitably brought the other with it'.

This bizarre blend of pathos and bathos, these quixotic changes of mood, were, in fact, as much a part of his personality as of his music. Bruno Walter wrote of his sudden and inexplicable shifts from gaiety to gloom. Likewise, Natalie Bauer-Lechner, a musician and another close and devoted friend of Mahler's until his marriage to Alma Schindler in 1902: 'I have never seen such a whirlwind succession of mood-changes in anyone else. His relationships with those nearest to him are at the mercy of this unpredictability. He can switch from the most passionate approval to the most violent disagreement without any transition whatever; and he can overwhelm you just as easily with unreasoning love as with unjust hatred'.

Perhaps the most fundamental influences upon Mahler's music were to be found in the very surroundings of his youth and amongst the literature for which he developed so insatiable an appetite from his earliest childhood. 'Des Knaben Wunderhorn' ('Youth's Magic Horn') — an anthology of German folk-poems something akin to the Grimm fairy tales in their quirky surrealist fantasies — was one work

Leopoldine and Justine Mahler, Mahler's sisters.

with which Mahler established a particularly close affinity in those early years. Its grotesque and fantastic images of dead soldiers responding to the roll-call, St. Anthony preaching to the fishes, a song contest between cuckoo and nightingale before an adjudicating donkey – were absolutely hypnotic to young Gustav. No doubt his feelings towards them were further intensified by the associations he was able to make in reality.

The town of Iglau (Jihlava), where the family were able to move on relaxation of certain Jewish restrictions and where his father first set up the distillery business, was full of such associations: the brazen military band strains emanating from the local barracks, Saturday night's raucous dance tunes, a wealth of regional folk music, and, most important of all, the richness, peace and tranquility of the surrounding countryside to which Mahler would always turn for a kind of spiritual purification. Nature was his refuge. It gave birth to the very sounds of his music: its inherent grandeur, its folkloric rusticity and, above all, its universality.

I have already seen the dew on the grasses – I am now so serenely gay and the tranquil happiness all around me is tip-toeing into my heart, too, as the sun of early spring lights up the wintery fields. Is spring awakening in my own breast?

Oh earth, my beloved earth, when, ah when, will you give refuge to him who is forsaken, receiving him back into your womb? Behold! Mankind has cast him out and he flees from its cold and heartless bosom, he flees to you alone! O take him, eternal, all-embracing mother, give a resting place to him who is without friend and without rest.

Few of Mahler's utterances, save the music itself, better convey his desperate need for escape from the sombre realities of his daily existence than the soul-baring letters from which those extracts were taken. Written when he was but eighteen, albeit a precocious eighteen, they crystalise an overwhelming awareness of his origins – an awareness that was to remain with him all his life. Little is known of the recipient – his sometime friend and walking companion, Joseph Steiner – save that he inexplicably diappeared from Mahler's life around 1879 and that it appears to have been through him that Mahler made the acquaintance of Gustav Schwarz, the estate supervisor of a nearby farm and a music lover of some perception. It was Schwarz, deeply impressed by young Gustav's keyboard prowess, who succeeded in persuading Bernard Mahler to encourage the boy's musical studies.

As we have seen, Bernard Mahler generally aspired to little more than a tyrannical domination of his household and a sound, hardworking business sense. Yet, in a strangely ironical way, it was he who formulated his son's destiny. Gustav showed an acute musical talent from the age of about four or five and, true to traditional romantic images of precocious young composers, he was to be found at his grandparents, improvising on an old piano in the attic. To Bernard Mahler's credit, though probably for no other reason than bettering his own status, he was prepared to make certain financial sacrifices in order that his son should take piano lessons. The ulterior motive was clear. Gustav would rise to become a performing piano 'virtuoso' and this in turn would reflect generously on his father's Jewish pride. Like many others of his kind, Bernard Mahler had great pretensions to learning. The odds may have been stacked hopelessly against him, but he never shrank from trying to better himself, socially and intellectually. After all, the pathway to success was paved with German culture and no matter how oppressively anti-semetism continued to restrict intellectual and social progress amongst the Jewish minority, it was up to individuals to rise above, or at least equal, the aspirations of their oppressors.

Gustav's early piano studies proceeded at phenominal speed (he later admitted to having dabbled in composition before mastering his keyboard scales). In 1870, on the 13th October at the age of ten, he gave his first public piano recital in Iglau. Its success was proof enough that Iglau was really too much of a backwater in which to develop his exceptional musical talents. Prague seemed a logical choice at the time, so it was there – to the *Gymnasium* – that Bernard sent his son, lodging him with the Grünfeld family (who owned a music shop and later produced one of the most famous pianists of the day – Alfred Grünfeld). There, it was also decided, he should simultaneously continue his piano studies. It was at this point that all progress in youg Gustav's early musical training came to an abrupt halt. The conditions to which the fragile eleven year old was subjected at the Grünfeld household were appalling, though by now, of course, he had come to endure most hardship in a kind of oblivious silent acceptance. Mercifully, Bernard Mahler, who still had some semblance of the protective paternal instinct about him, so say nothing of the wasted fees he could envisage, very soon learned of his son's predicament and angrily whisked him back home.

Events moved rapidly now. The aforementioned meeting with Gustav Schwarz set the wheels in motion and Bernard Mahler was quickly convinced, without too much ado, that the Vienna Conservatory was the only place for his son. Schwarz, it seems, took Gustav to Joseph Epstein, Professor of Pianoforte at the Conservatory, and Epstein's reaction was instantaneous: 'He is a born musician . . . I cannot possibly be wrong'. Thirty-six years later, Epstein could still recall the gratitude in young Mahler's eyes at that moment. Vienna was about to cast its spell.

# 2. The Vienna Conservatory

The Vienna of 1875 must have been bewildering to this small, pale and somewhat awkward youth from the provinces. Mahler was only fifteen when he entered the Conservatory in September of that year and there it stood: glittering capital of the Austro-Hungarian Empire and possibly the most famous city in the whole of central Europe. Bigoted old values were dying hard but there was unquestionably a smell of change in the air. Clashes between old and new, symbolised in music by the ferocious antagonism between supporters of Brahms on the one hand and Wagner on the other, were rapidly coming to a head. Already the radical upheaval in the arts that was to bring about the 'Secession' renaissance at the turn of the century was clearly in sight. Mahler had arrived at a stimulating but difficult time.

Principal of the Conservatory from 1851-1893 was the legendary and wildly eccentric public figure of Joseph Hellmesberger who it is said harboured three major dislikes: Jacob Grun, his successor as leader of the Vienna Philharmonic, short-sighted people, and Jews. Mahler's other teachers at the time were Julius Epstein, for piano, Robert Fuchs, for harmony, and Franz Krenn, for composition. It was Fuchs who told Alma Mahler years later: 'Mahler always played truant and yet there was nothing he couldn't do'. Composition dominated his student activities. According to Alma, as a composer of songs he was soon drawing the accolade of 'another Schubert' from many of those around him. His instrumental projects were as yet less successful, although he did later express some regret at having scrapped so much of this earlier material, singling out a Piano Quartet of which he was particularly fond. A projected first symphony went the way of a piano suite on account of Hellmesberger's refusal to conduct it using Mahler's hand-written parts. Naturally, it was financially out of the question for Mahler to have them professionally copied, and in his exhaustive efforts to have them ready in time, mistakes had crept into the copies. Financial hardship was, of course, a perpetual headache for the majority of students at the Conservatory, though Mahler, absorbed as he always was in his compositional pursuits,

Mahler, 1878.

17

was generally oblivious to the near poverty-level of his surroundings, retreating whenever possible into his own private world of daydreams.

Sharing this frugal existence were some pretty remarkable fellow students; most notably, Hugo Wolf (who later degenerated into insanity after an unfortunate rift with Mahler), Hans Rott (also to die insane – a comment on the times if ever there was one), and Rudolf Krzyzanowski who was Mahler's closest friend during this period. The Wolf/Mahler rift came about, in the first instance, over the libretto for a fairy-tale opera *Rübezahl* which both were anxious to work on and both, in fact, did – except that Mahler did so unbeknown to his friend and in the space of only a few hours! Wolf, who had barely made a start by this time, was deeply offended by what he saw as an act of flagrant deceit on Mahler's part. He had, after all, confided in Mahler over the original idea. Ironically, neither party ever completed the project, but it crippled their friendship.

Compared with others in this select circle, Mahler was perhaps the most fortunate. He had an income of sorts from piano teaching and his parents kept him well stocked with parcels of food and clothing from home. Even so, he was extremely poor. Only one year after arriving he made a request to the Conservatory to be excused

*Top* Julius Epstein, Mahler's piano teacher at The Vienna Conservatory.
*Bottom* The eccentric Joseph Hellsmesberger, principal of The Vienna Conservatory from 1851-1893. Oil painting by Wilhelm Vita.

*Left* Hugo Wolf at the time when he was a fellow student with Mahler at The Vienna Conservatory.
*Right* Heinrich Krzyanowski, Mahler's closest friend during his term at The Vienna Conservatory.

his fees, at which point Epstein stepped in with an offer to pay half of everything due from then onwards and assist too in the ever-problematical search for the pupils which were then providing Gustav and his colleagues with their daily bread and butter.

In a perverse sort of way, it was partly hardship that bound Wolf, Krzyzanowski and Mahler together when they eventually shared lodgings. They shared, too, an understanding of each other's creative problems and, as we shall see, a joint idolisation of their God, Richard Wagner, and demi-God, Anton Bruckner.

Antagonism between the Wagner/Brahms factions cannot be overestimated. Here was a division in Viennese musical circles between which there could be no neutrality. Society was split on every level. Wagner had grown inexorably to become champion of the progressive youth while Brahms remained the respected pillar of conservatism, despite the music itself, which continued to delve into areas far beyond so demeaning a label. The student sect were, of course, deeply under the influence of Wagner's elusive spell and his visit to Vienna in the winter of 1875 to supervise productions of *Tannhäuser* and *Lohengrin* was inevitably one of the highlights of Mahler's first term at the conservatory. Wagner being second only to Beethoven in Mahler's eyes, these feelings of adulation and devotion might best be summed up in one of his own remarks: 'When Wagner has spoken, one can only keep silent'.

Then there was Anton Bruckner: the humble genius whom

Mahler and his student friends forever witnessed falling foul of the critical powers-to-be; destructive figures like Edward Hanslick, the ringleader of a perpetual barrage against Wagner and, eventually, Mahler himself. To watch Bruckner rising above these bitter condemnations with dignity, determination and, above all, unshakeable faith in the honesty of his own creative utterances, was one spiritual lesson that undoubtedly helped to sustain Mahler through many of his own early rejections. Bruckner never 'sold out' to those who sought to change his ways and destroy his individuality. Neither would Mahler.

Bruckner was 52 years of age at this time and, in spite of all Hanslick's attempts to keep him out, lecturer of harmony and counterpoint at the university. Mahler never actually studied with him but would attend his lectures whenever possible and spend a good deal of time, socially, in his company along with Wolf, Rott (a special favourite of Bruckner's) and others. It was Bruckner who related to them a magical account of his pilgrimage to Bayreuth for the very first complete cycle of Wagner's *Der Ring Des Nibelungen* in 1876 and whose warm-hearted encouragement and generous counsel was always on hand as a constant source of inspiration.

It was the first performance of his Third Symphony that finally secured, between him and Mahler, an inseparable bond that was to permanently link them from then onwards. The occasion was nothing short of total disaster. Orchestral sabotage and audience abuse gradually emptied the hall leaving only a handful of admirers, Mahler among them. Bruckner's depression at the cruelty and malevolence of the whole event was at least partly alleviated by publisher Theodor Rattig's decision to publish the score (the first of Bruckner's ever to be published) in full and piano-reduction editions. Rattig had attended both the rehearsals and catastrophic première and somehow, despite the chaotic results brought about as a direct result of the orchestra's disinterest, he was able to catch sight of the work's creative spark. Mahler and Kryzanowski were entrusted with the task of preparing the piano reduction. Both were a mere 17 years old then and their supportive enthusiasm turned the whole project into a labour of love and good faith. Delighted with the finished product, Bruckner gave the manuscript of the second version to Mahler. Some 25 years later, when Mahler had arrived at the peak of his fame as 'monarch' of the Vienna State Opera, he waived the royalties on his first four symphonies in order that his own publisher, Universal Edition, could take over responsibility for Bruckner's music.

Mahler graduated from the Conservatory in July 1878 with his diploma and a string of prizes for piano playing. The reality of finding his own way in the professional musical world was suddenly upon him. Decisions had to be made. He had already abandoned

Anton Bruckner.

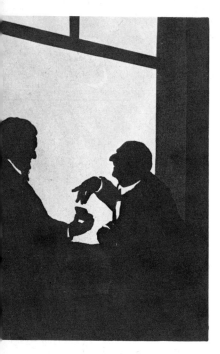

A silhouette caricature of
Wagner and Bruckner.

any thoughts of a pianistic career. Seeing both Liszt and Anton Rubenstein perform in the same year (1877) had convinced him that he had neither the skill nor the stature to truly succeed as a concert performer. Even conducting appears not to have become a serious consideration by then. It had no place on the regular curriculum at the Conservatory and Mahler's only orchestral participation up to that point had been with the Conservatory orchestra as timpanist. Everything but composition was still very far from his mind. He had already begun work on a dramatic cantata *Das Klagende Lied* ('Song of Lamentation' – its text, a poem of his own making) and would continue with that before returning to Vienna in the autumn for further lectures, further teaching and still more poverty. If Mahler moved lodgings once, he moved twenty times. It was a period of great depression but, as it turned out, some intellectual compensation.

Very much in keeping with the artistic trends and pretentions of the day, Mahler, along with his room-mates Wolf and Kryzanowski, became involved with a socialist movement known as the Pernerstorfer Circle. Hand in hand with the fashionable trappings of political awareness and, of course, vegetarianism, this motley group of high-school and university students immersed themselves in the writings of the great thinkers of the day; above all, Nietzsche, to whom Mahler would turn again and again for inspiration. His introduction to the movement came via a young Jewish poet, Siegfried Lipiner, whose philosophy and seemingly boundless knowledge made a profound and lasting impression on Mahler. The association was to continue for many years.

The summer of 1879 was spent in Hungary, as a family piano tutor, and at home in Iglau where Mahler became hopelessly infatuated – for the first time, it seems – by Josephine Poisl, a postmaster's daughter who was one of his pupils at the time. It was a short and hapless relationship but one that produced, from his depression, three songs and a renewal of activity towards both further composition and his humble beginnings as a conductor. Realising that he could no longer viably continue in his 'eternal student' guise, Mahler turned to the publisher Rattig for whom he had produced the piano reduction of Bruckner's Third Symphony. Rattig suggested that he find himself an agent and promptly put him in touch with Gustav Löwy. Löwy accepted Mahler as a client on agreement of a five per-cent commission deal and, in fact, went on to represent him for nearly ten years.

Bad Hall was the appropriately named summer resort where Mahler began his apprenticeship into what he justifiably described later, when thinking back to these early experiences, as 'the hell of the theatre'. A tiny wooden structure seating about 200, the theatre at Bad Hall was rendered uninhabitable every time it rained. Like

each of the positions that were to demean his talent during those early days, Mahler found himself acting as conductor, stage manager, administrator, librarian and porter at one and the same time. There is no question that the likes of such engagements provided invaluable grass-roots experience in every conceivable aspect of operatic theatre, but since this was never the course that Mahler had envisaged for a career in the first place, one can appreciate his double frustration.

Löwy was soon anxiously instructed to be on the look out for a new position for Gustav, and meanwhile, during the winter months, Mahler returned to Vienna where he continued work on his cantata, *Das Klagende Lied.* By November 1st of that year, 1880, it was complete – his first sizeable opus (though one shouldn't perhaps overlook a *Nordic Symphony* – later destroyed – also from this period) and one for which the prospect of a major première seemed at the time to be the perfect formula for establishing his credentials as a composer. To this end he decided to compete for the Beethoven Prize of the Gesellschaft der Musikfreunde, instituted in 1875, and open to past and present Conservatory students. But it just wasn't to be. That the jury included Brahms, Hans Richter (revered Musical Director of the Imperial Opera), Carl Goldmark and Joseph Hellmesberger was enough to ensure that his boldly innovative piece stood little or no chance of success: 'If the Conservatory jury had given me the Beethoven prize of 600 gulden, my whole life would have taken a different course. I would not have had to go to Laibach and perhaps would have thus been spared the whole vile operatic career'.

*Top* The primitive theatre at Bad Hall where Mahler first conducted.
*Bottom* Gustav Löwy, Mahler's first agent.

Mahler, 1881.

# 3. Laibach Olmütz Kassel

Whether or not Mahler's total disillusionment with the operatic theatre during his first menial experiences of it played any part in his eventually eschewing all serious thoughts of composing for the medium remains one area open to a certain amount of speculation. There is no doubt that he resented the amount of time that he was forced to spend in the opera house, for all the characteristic endeavour that he brought to his work there. On the other hand, he realised that here was a means of keeping himself closely in touch with the mechanics of music. The practical would feed the creative. By working with orchestral musicians and singers, on whatever level, he would encounter most of the problems ever likely to beset the interpreter and consequently never find himself working in a vacuum, as it were.

Though he would doubtless have never acknowledged the fact at the time, Mahler was lucky to have been born into a period when every city in western and central Europe boasted an opera house of sorts. Such institutions had become the established centres of artistic life in each district. An entire family might spend an evening in the company of opera, operetta or dance. Standards

*Right*
Laibach.

25

The Royal Municipal
Theatre, Olmütz.

varied enormously as we shall see – sometimes down to the lower
depths of pure ridicule – but quite often, up and coming young
artists from all parts of the globe (America, for instance) would
travel great distances in order to attach themselves to such
companies if only for the sheer range of experience that they
offered.

During 1881 and 1882, hot on the heels of his withering
experiences in Bad Hall, Mahler's agent secured engagements for
him at Laibach and Olmütz: small, modest companies both situated
in Moravia and both subject to the same extensive inadequacies that
he was beginning to think would blight any and every contact he
was ever likely to make with the theatre. Even then, he was by
nature, a perfectionist. That he was working with inexperienced,
often sub-standard artists, tiny orchestras and virtually no
production resources, save those created by his own hand, didn't
deter him in the least. Ambition and determination spurred him on
into making the best of a bad lot. A number of highly suspect, but
nonetheless amusing, anecdotes have been passed down relating to
this whole period: how, on one occasion, he was forced into
whistling 'The Last Rose of Summer' in Flotow's *Martha* when a
singer failed to appear on stage or how, on another, he found
himself with only one single member of the male chorus for the
'Soldiers Chorus' in Gounod's *Faust* and he, for some reason,
sauntering across the stage singing the Lutheran chorale, 'Ein Feste
Burg'!

The season at the Laibach Landestheater lasted for six months

26

from September to April and, at the very least, Mahler could console himself with a reasonably civilised and varied repertoire which included: Verdi's *Il Travatore*, Gounod's *Faust*, Mozart's *Die Zauberflöte*, Flotow's *Martha* and Weber's *Die Freischutz*. No such consolation could be drawn from Olmütz. The repertoire there consisted almost entirely of Meyerbeer and Verdi though, under the circumstances, that in itself was perhaps a blessing in disguise. In January 1883, angered and appalled by the whole set up, Mahler wrote to his new friend Friedrich Löhr: a philologist. Löhr and Mahler grew very close over this period. Löhr, in fact, emerged as the major recipient of Mahler's most revealing letters over the next few years.

'I am paralysed, like one who has just fallen to earth from heaven. ever since I entered the Olmütz Theater, I have felt like a man who is awaiting the last judgement. When a noble steed is harnessed with oxen to a cart, he has no choice but to pull and sweat with them. I scarcely dare to appear before you, I feel so covered with filth . . . I am almost always alone except during rehearsals. Up to now, thank God, I have conducted nothing but Meyerbeer and Verdi. I have successfully plotted against including Wagner and Mozart in the repertoire as I could not bear to massacre 'Lohengrin' or 'Don Giovanni' here . . .'

On February 13th news of Wagner's death reached Olmütz. Mahler was crushed by a profound sense of loss. Only his sheer professionalism enabled him to continue with the drudgery at hand. Suddenly it all seemed so much worse.

Vienna came like a breath of spring after Olmütz. Mahler had grown a beard in an attempt, no doubt, to emulate greater physical maturity and his agent Löwy was again in search of a new position for him. A number of early compositions were in progress. None saw completion. Friedrich Eckstein, who was with him at the Conservatory, describes him more fully at this time:

'Already in the curiously wagging manner of his gait, his unusual irritability manifested itself. His tense and intellectual face, thin and extremely mobile, was framed by a full brown beard; his speech was pointed with a strongly Austrian intonation. He invariably carried a parcel of books under his arm'.

It was an enthusiastic letter of commendation from one, Karl Überhorst, chief stage director at the Dresden Court Opera, which finally secured Mahler's next position as second conductor at the Royal Prussian Court Theatre in Kassel, Germany. Überhorst had observed him in action at Olmütz and while he wasn't one hundred per-cent certain that the young Austrian was yet ready for the dignities of his own house, he was nonetheless impressed by his

The Royal Theatre, Kassel.

ability to obtain good results from indifferent material. In the event, Kassel turned out to be a very long way from the proverbial dream-come-true that Mahler might have envisaged.

The resources there were indeed infinitely superior to anything he had experienced before. There was a chorus of thirty-eight, an orchestra of forty-nine and a regular pool of professional singers. His elaborate title, 'Royal Musical and Choral Director', however, was not at all what it implied. Mahler was entirely answerable to the Principal Conductor, Wilhelm Treiber, and he was apt to run the establishment along the lines of a Prussian military school. Reports were made on all rehearsals and those involving a female singer could only be held in the presence of a third party. All cuts were to be reported and misdemeanours such as lateness or loss of temper were duly noted in a black book. As for repertoire, Treiber, of course, commandeered pretty well everything of substance and Mahler was relegated to doing what he could with French, Italian and lesser German stock – Flotow and Lortzing, for instance. 'Music for special occasions' was another of his designations. Kassel's 'second' conductor was obliged to compose that, as required.

In January, 1884, just as Mahler's disillusionment with the Court Opera was deepening still further, a muscial event took place in Kassel which would significantly influence, both directly and indirectly, the course of his life over the next few years. The world renowned conductor, Hans von Bülow, arrived in town for one concert and Mahler was instantly spellbound by his artistry. Bülow, to whom Wagner had originally assigned the premières of both *Die Meistersinger* and *Tristan und Isolde*, was previously married to Liszt's daughter, Cosima, until Wagner lured her away to mistresshood and, later, marriage. His allegiance, not surprisingly, had then switched sharply towards Brahms and it was as an interpreter of his music that he was then perhaps best known.

Impressionable and impetuous, Mahler unwisely felt that he had nothing to lose by approaching Bülow to accept him as a pupil: anything to extricate himself from his miserable and unprogressive plight in Kassel. The letter he wrote, though, was both hysterical and ill-considered. Bülow passed the letter to Treiber. Treiber

Hans von Bülow.

passed it to the Director, Herr Gilsa, and Mahler's position at Kassel became intolerable. Worse than that, Gilsa, who was now becoming increasingly aware of his young second conductor's potential, was not about to let him go in a hurry. For the time being anyway, he was trapped.

The summer brought sustenance. Bayreuth were staging memorial performances of *Parsifal*, the first since Wagner's death, and Mahler decided to make the pilgrimage – his first. A letter to Friedrich Löhr crystalises those impressions:

I can hardly describe my present state to you. When I came out of the Festspielhaus, completely spellbound, I understood that the greatest and most painful revelation had just been made to me, and that I would carry it with me unspoiled all my life.

One other incident, the following year, acted as a significant diversion while the search went on for a way out of his predicament. Mahler became passionately involved with a young singer, Johanna Richter. Their relationship was doomed from the start but it did inspire what was to be Mahler's first masterpiece – the song cycle, *Lieder eines fahrenden Gesellen* ('Songs of a Wayfarer' – completed in 1884): a poignant reflection of the solitude he now experienced as a result of his own wanderings, to say nothing of the miseries he was enduring in Kassel. Thematic material from these songs would also be utilised to great effect in his First Symphony.

Kassel, however, was yet to provide one shining light in an otherwise gloomy period. From June 29th to July 1st, 1885, a music festival of its own was planned and Mahler had been named as Musical Director. Mendelssohn's oratorio *St. Paul* and Beethoven's Ninth Symphony had been selected as the main works and, in addition to the opera orchestra, four choral societies were to be involved. It was unquestionably a major event in the Kassel musical calendar and one which Principal Conductor Treiber felt most strongly should have been placed in his charge. Furious at this apparent usurping of his position, he demanded from Director Gilsa that Mahler be taken off the project. By now, however, Mahler had learned from Löwy of a timely offer from the prestigious Leipzig Opera (again at the instigation of Überhorst in Dresden) and acting upon the security of his future he was able to dig in his heels. The Kassel festival was important to him. He was determined that Treiber would not deprive him of it.

What ensued then was as ugly an example of Germany's unspoken anti-semitism as Mahler had yet experienced. Treiber, who had at that point been delegated responsibility for a number of rehearsals, began spreading resentment in the orchestra that while he did all the work, a Jew would be basking in the glory. Under pressure, the theatre orchestra refused to participate and Mahler was faced with the dilemma of how on earth he was going to raise the requisite number of players in time. Never one to admit defeat, he scoured Germany for musicians until he had drawn together his full complement. A band of local infantry were even thrown in for good measure. The end result was an absolute triumph. Rehearsals had been ruthlessly demanding but players and singers found themselves surpassing standards they had previously thought unattainable. Germany had caught its first glimpse of the blinding talent that was shortly to take the world by storm. Overnight, Mahler was the man of the hour. Kassel had no alternative but to accept the fact that it could hold him no longer.

By mutual consent, his contract was prematurely terminated. Mahler was both relieved and elated. With one year still to run before the start of his Leipzig committment he decided to approach Angelo Neumann of the ailing German Theatre in Prague for an engagement which might bridge the hiatus.

Mahler, 1884.

# 4. Prague Leipzig

What began as something of a stop-gap grew into perhaps the single most intense period of development in Mahler's early career. Prague was desperately in need of rejuvenation when he arrived there in 1885, and its Intendant, Angelo Neumann, an ex-singer and shrewd business administrator, was quick to recognise the vital signs and take his chances on what was, after all, still very much an unknown commodity. Mahler's notoriety had not yet permeated too far beyond the confines of the small provincial houses where he felt as though he had been languishing forever.

No sooner had he arrived in Prague when changing circumstances brought him into practical contact with the music of his beloved Wagner for the very first time. The dream that had begun in Bayreuth, and would soon lead to the setting of new standards in operatic production throughout Europe, unexpectedly began to be realised when Principal Conductor, Anton Seidl, whose fame had been spreading as far afield as America at this time, was offered a post at the Metropolitan in New York. Ludwig Slansky, the other chief conductor at Prague, was perfectly agreeable, it seems, to pass on as much as possible of the work load to his younger colleague, and so Mahler found himself in a unique and highly desirable position of authority. In the December of that year he was assigned responsibility for the two principal new productions of the season: *Das Rheingold* and *Die Walküre* – both, ironically, using the Bayreuth settings. A new production of Mozart's *Don Giovanni* followed shortly when Slansky decided to decline it on the grounds that the opera had never been a success in the city (strange when one considers that, like Symphony No. 38 – subtitled after the city – it was for Prague that the opera was written). Mahler was overjoyed. His repertoire was going from strength to strength and with it his reputation. Wagner's *Die Meistersinger* and *Tannhäuser*, Beethoven's *Fidelio* and the Ninth Symphony all figured prominently during the course of that first year.

Not all the critics approved of Mahler's distinctly individual and, as such, controversial way on the rostrum and, of course, there was

33

always bound to be one, as Mahler went on to discover, who would make it his business to conduct a campaign of personal antagonism against him. Neumann himself had confessed to being distracted by the exaggerated and fidgety gestures that typified Mahler's work at this stage of his career. As a conductor, Mahler's interpretive qualities reached out well beyond the accepted classical conventions of the time. He was eccentric in his youth but exciting and unpredictable in a way that many of the dull, traditional 'time-beaters' were not. By all accounts there was an expressive intensity about his work then. Extremes of dynamics and wild tempo fluctuations were part and parcel of a profound temperament. He often strayed from the letter of the score but nonetheless made it his business to serve the composer's aesthetic intentions as best he knew how. The means to the end was invariably wayward but, by all accounts, his insight was almost always revelationary. Fortunately there were those who welcomed hearing great music through new ears, as it were. Equally, though, there were those who resented the merest hint of what might be considered tampering with accepted values. These factions were the bain of Mahler's entire life as both composer and conductor.

Prague, then, had turned out to be such a success that Mahler began to wonder if he would live to regret his perhaps rash decision to accept the engagement at Leipzig. In all but name he was Principal Conductor in Prague. He felt at home there: an Austrian – not a German-speaking stranger in an alien land. Leipzig, on the other hand, was dominated by one of the great conducting names of the day – Arthur Nikisch – and it seemed unlikely that, as second conductor, Mahler would exert very much artistic pull at all. The Prague experience had given him his first taste of artistic freedom. He realised now just how important that was. But this was all speculation. It was too late to retract from the Leipzig contract now and foolhardy to suppose that the powers-to-be there would consider releasing him. News of Mahler's successes were spreading far and wide now. He definitely had some cachet.

For a while the advantages at Leipzig far outweighed the disadvantages. Any fears he might have had seemed groundless. In the first place, here was one of Germany's major houses: a luxurious 1900-seat theatre built to accommodate productions on the grandest scale and run with civilised efficiency by Max Stägermann, the company's amiable Intendant. It boasted one of the finest house orchestras in Europe – a staggering seventy-six regular players as against fifty-two in Prague (at least one imagines this is how Mahler would have reacted to his increased personnel) and facilities that at last began to approach the level of excellence that Mahler hoped might one day be placed entirely at his disposal. Then there was Leipzig itself – a fine old Saxon city steeped in

Arthur Nikisch.

The Leipzig Opera.

musical history: Wagner's birthplace, centre of the music world's most important publishers and home of the famous Gewandhaus concerts, founded by Robert Schumann in 1834 and supervised by Felix Mendelssohn from 1835-43.

Initially, Nikisch was not ungenerous with repertoire. During the first two months following his arrival Mahler was entrusted with Wagner's *Lohengrin* and *Rienzi*, Weber's *Der Freischütz*, Halevy's *La Juivre* and Mozart's *Die Zauberflöte*. Again, there were the usual objections from certain critical quarters as to the uncompromising nature of his readings, but by and large the response to his work was enthusiastic. Nikisch himself was the first to commend and encourage him which seemed to be a step in the right direction, while so far the company were showing him the kind of respect and co-operation that did not always come as a matter of course. Whichever way one looks at it, Mahler *was* a taskmaster. Malice, pure and simple, played no part in his make-up but he would go to any lengths in his efforts to achieve perfection. Basically, he cared very deeply about the music he conducted just as if it were his own. Good was not good enough. Complacency and defeatism in any shape or form were simply an anathema to him. If bettering one single phrase meant victimising a player beyond what might normally be considered reasonable, then he would go ahead and do so. He could not actually understand weakness in subordinates.

35

Consequently, if he sensed inferiority the chances are that he would
home in on it. He certainly did not suffer fools gladly but, by the
same token, bore no grudges when all was said and forgotten. There
are a great many hair-raising stories which tell of Mahler at his most
tyrannical: his temperamental authoritarianism, his despotism,
even his satanism – enough, in fact, to all but fill the pages of this
book – but no less illuminating are the stories which tell of his good
humour, his smiling affability with players and, more to the point,
his musical perception, miraculous ear and technical mastery.
There were no in-betweens. Those who shared his ideals had, as
one New York Philharmonic player later put it, 'nothing to fear'.
To them, he was the answer to a prayer.

Inevitably, Mahler was not content to allow his comfortable

36

position in Leipzig to drift on indefinitely without showing some signs of positive progress; and none appeared to be forthcoming. Nikisch continued to allocate only the early Wagner in the repertoire and Stägermann, prompted by a growing public demand for Mahler's work but loathe to override the older man's seniority for fear of deeply offending him, began making promises that he could not possibly hope to keep. To pacify Mahler, for instance, he pledged that the next *Ring* cycle would be shared between them, only to find that Nikisch was unwilling. Mahler's artistic pride was undergoing too much stress. Playing second fiddle to Nikisch was not part of his ambitious plan.

Early in 1887, however, just as he was in the throes of looking elsewhere again (Hamburg, Karlsruhe and Prague, of course, had all expressed interest), Nikisch fell seriously ill. Suddenly, he found himself saddled with the entire repertoire. It was a welcome burden but one that even his insatiable energy was hard pushed to meet. New productions of *Die Walküre* and *Siegfried* followed each other in quick succession. Public acclaim was running high but the press were less sure.

Nikisch's illness was to be a lengthy business. During the 1887-88 season Mahler conducted over two hundred performances of fifty-four operas. That gives us some idea of his stamina and determination. Add to this yet another illicit femal distraction and one is left marvelling at his fortitude.

His torrid affair with the wife of Carl Weber's grandson, Marion Mathilda von Weber, seven years his senior, came so close to becoming a public scandal that they actually planned to elope. Gustav's feelings of distress were no doubt mingled with a sense of relief, though, when his paramour failed to appear at the appointed time. He simply could not afford to risk putting his career in jeopardy at this of all times. His ailing and problematical family were totally dependent upon his success for their survival. Morally and financially he was their only source of support. Sister Justine, then only seventeen – a spendthrift and something of a borderline case mentally – was barely capable of running a household in which both mother and father were becoming weaker by the minute. The education and welfare of the other surviving brothers and sisters were a major responsibility too: one which Gustav was again expected to shoulder. Emma was the youngest at ten. Otto (Mahler's favourite) at twelve, was musically quite talented but already neurotic and lazy, too; tragically he would eventually die by his own hand. Sister Leopoldine, the next oldest to Gustav, would be dead in three years from a brain tumour and Alois, Gustav's nineteen year old brother, was generally deceitful and never up to much good. It constantly depressed Mahler that his inherent selfishness and obsessional commitment to work often stood

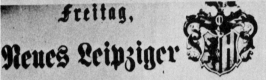

Poster for the premiere of Weber's opera *Die Drei Pinto's*, successfully completed by Mahler.

between him and his love for those closest to him. Never, though, did he shirk his family responsibilities.

Mahler's affair with Frau Weber did, as it happened, produce something of consequence: his one and only foray, of sorts, into operatic composition. Carl von Weber approached him about completing, or rather reconstructing, his grandfather's comic opera, *Die Drei Pintos*, which existed only in a set of extremely scanty notes and sketches. Mahler's subsequent success with the project, accepted partly out of admiration for it's composer and rather more out of a desire to be closer to his new-found amour, brought him enormous acclaim, not only in Leipzig, where he conducted the premiere in January 1885, but later in Vienna, too.

By 1888, rumours that Nikisch might be considering a move to the Royal Opera, Budapest, had come to naught. He was still too weak to contemplate a decent share of the work load and Mahler was growing increasingly weary of carrying what amounted to the full artistic burden in Nikisch's shadow. Schedules at the theatre were also beginning to eat into his precious composition time and that bothered him more than anything. For the first time in his career Mahler found his creative efforts at direct odds with his theatrical duties. Come December 1888 he was hard at work on two projects: an extended symphonic poem subtitled *Titan* after Jean Paul Richter's novel, later to emerge as the First Symphony, and a monumental funeral march entitled *Totenfeier* which would eventually constitute the first movement of his Second Symphony.

Stägermann was justifiably growing concerned. He understood Mahler's priorities. He understood, too, that it was unreasonable to expect an artist of Mahler's calibre to adopt a realistic commitment to the company when there was no little or no hope for his advancement there. Regretably, but on good terms, they parted company.

Ironically, it was at Budapest that Mahler, and not Nikisch, took up his sixth and most influential position to date.

# 5. Budapest

Nationalistic feeling was running high in Hungary during the latter part of the 19th Century. Ceaseless agitation from Hungarian factions within the Monarchy had gradually brought about some improvement in their political status, but the climate was still one of uncertainty. As a symbol, then, of Hungary's nationalistic pride, the Budapest Opera was an institution of the utmost significance; she badly needed to assert her cultural heritage in the light of ever diminishing political security. Built only in 1884, this was one of the most technically advanced theatres of its time: a magnificent 1200-seater equipped with the latest in hydraulic stage machinery and blessed with superb acoustics. The potential was enormous and yet by 1888, only four years after its inception, mis-management and a general lack of artistic flair had already brought it to the brink of financial disaster.

In January 1888, Baron Franz von Beniczky, a cultured aristocrat of no musical experience, was installed to assess the damage. One problem area was immediately apparent. The comings and goings of countless guest artists was having a crippling effect on the budgets while the regular pool of contract artists were barely capable of undertaking even secondary roles. In other words, the ensemble was non-existent. Plainly a dynamic and resourceful chief conductor and artistic director was now crucial towards revitalising standards, re-establshing prestige and bringing audiences back into the house.

Beniczky had heard about Gustav Mahler. It was possible that this 28 year old with accolades coming in from all over Europe, and reputedly a sharp administrative ability to match that of his musicianship, might well be the answer to his problems. He engaged Mahler later in 1888 by way of a cautiously worded contract which placed particular emphasis on the nationalistic requirements of the house and specified that he would be expected to acquire a thorough knowledge of the Hungarian language (with which Mahler was totally unfamiliar!). Even so, Beniczky had not bargained for the obstructive tactics of certain nationalistic bigots who resented the prospect of an 'outsider' taking control of their

*Opposite* Mahler, 1892.

*Bottom* Baron von Beniczky.

41

The Royal Opera, Budapest.

national institution, however productive his talents might prove to be. At the forefront of their ranks were Ferenz Erkel, then a celebrated composer and leader of the National School of Opera, and the one-armed, sometime-composer, Count Geza von Zichy, of whose work Emperor Franz Joseph was reputed to have said: 'I was at Count Zichy's opera . . . a lively ballet kept me from falling asleep'. It was Zichy who would eventually take control of the opera.

Budapest was a dazzling offer for Mahler. As director of a sizeable house with absolutely unlimited powers, his position had elevated dramatically since Leipzig. It did not matter that the Royal Opera was run-down and badly in need of complete artistic restructuring. Those prospects excited him. It was a challenge. For the first time in his career he had sole control over both musical and administrative matters. He could build his own company from scratch and experiment with a few of the concepts of 'total theatre' that he had dreamed about for so long.

First priority was to rid the house of the 'guest star' system that it had been struggling to maintain for too long. A strong national company was needed: young, energetic artists prepared to work hard on the development of their talents and, more important still, make a commitment to one house. It is interesting to note here just how much of an obssession with operatic 'personalities' had grown throughout Europe during this period. Even in Vienna, it was a relatively common occurrence for an opera to be given in several languages simultaneously depending upon the nationality of the

42

Count Geza von Zichy.

principals and their laziness or reluctance to learn the role in the original tongue. A successful house, in fact, was to a large extent dependent upon who, rather than what, was being sung. Production values were falling and that was one area in which Mahler was fully determined to put matters to rights at Budapest.

Within three months of his arrival, totally undaunted by the language problems, he had staged trimphant new productions – in Hungarian – of *Das Rheingold* and *Die Walküre*. Acting styles were already showing signs of becoming more fluid at his insistence. It mattered to Mahler that some semblance of belief was created in the characters of the on-stage drama just as it mattered that the scenic aspects of operatic staging should progress, not regress. He began using all the sophisticated technical facilities at his disposal. Evocative back-projections replaced futile attempts at stage realism: the Valkyries' horses in the last act of *Die Walküre*, for example. Visual innovations were cropping up everywhere.

In addition to Wagner, Mozart naturally figured prominently in his initial plans. A completely re-vamped *Marriage of Figaro* was followed later, in 1890, by a rapturously received production of *Don Giovanni* which apparently prompted Brahms to declare that 'to hear a true "Giovanni" one should hear it in Budapest'. Again, every performance was given in Hungarian. The purists sneered, of course, but Mahler knew that only in this way could he hope to lure the Hungarian music lover back into the theatre and at the same time overcome some of the scepticism levelled against his own nationality. He was right, of course. Standards were rising, profits were rising, and as a result, public admiration and support had never been greater. All the more extraordinary, then, that the nationalists' anti-Mahler campaign should have intensified during the second year of his contract.

Mahler was dismayed. In spite of all his efforts, he was accused of fostering only German interests in his choice of repertoire. The plain truth was that there simply weren't any new Hungarian works of substance being written at the time. He had considered Ferenz Erkel's opera *Brankovics Gyorgy* worthy of a production, but generally his feeling was that the public were far better served by sticking to the best of the established repertoire. And the public appeared to agree. There were occasional little diversions once he felt that his audiences were ready to experiment. New trends in the 'verismo' style from Italy to some extent fascinated him and Mascagni's *Cavalleria Rusticana* actually made more of a world-wide impact when Mahler presented it in December 1890 than it did at its Rome première shortly before.

Public support for his achievements, though, did not stop the nationalistic antagonism growing, and as it did, Mahler began thirsting again for his roots. German opera: in German.

1889 was a very painful year. His father, ailing for so long, finally died on February 18th, and both his mother and sister Leopoldine passed away later in the same year. It seems that he was not even able to attend his own mother's funeral such was the pressure of responsibility in Budapest at the time. In a strangely callous and compulsive sort of way Mahler's commitment to work would always take precedence over personal considerations. Nonetheless, this was one decision that pained him deeply. His friend, Friedrich Löhr took his place. They had become even closer during Easter of that year. Löhr had visited him in Budapest and together they had spent time walking by the Danube, discussing initial sketches for the second symphony and generally trying to ease the strain that was beginning to show in Mahler on account of his mother's fast fading health and the irritations in Budapest.

Following his mother's death, Justine moved in with Mahler for a while. Both were in need of recuperation. He had undergone

*Top left* Archaeologist, Friedrich Löhr, an intimate friend of Mahler's during the 1880s and 1890s.

*Bottom* 'The Huntsman's Funeral', a children's engraving by Moritz von Schwind which was Mahler's inspiration for the Funeral March in the First Symphony.

painful surgery for haemorrhoids in the summer and she was spiritually and physically crushed by the build up of family tragedy. November 20th saw the première of what we now know as the First Symphony: then in its extended five-movement form as a symphonic poem.

This was the first public hearing of any of Mahler's orchestral works and if the reception in the hall was cool to say the least, the effect on some of the critics was devastating. Its musical language was so new as to be alien to them. They understood neither its rarified atmospheres nor bizarre ironies: the sounds of nature awakening from stillness into the dawn, for example, distilled at the opening of the work into a sustained seven-octave-deep A in the strings overlaid with faint trumpet calls and isolated bird songs; or the quirky and sardonic third movement funeral march inspired by a well known Austrian childrens' engraving, 'The Huntsman's Funeral', where forest animals are depicted accompanying the dead

huntsman's coffin to the grave. The instrumental timbres in this movement were quite revolutionary at the time. In places, Mahler had deliberately scored for instruments whose essential sound character was unsuitable for the material in hand, or else pushed them to an extreme or strained part of their range in order to accentuate the grotesque ironies in the music. Established here, in fact, were all the future hallmarks of his orchestration, allied as they were to so many childhood influences: the vulgar village bands, the rustic folk melodies, the sights and sounds of nature. He even introduced a stroke of unexpected bravado at the triumphant close of the piece with a request in the score that the seven horns (or eight as it usually is) stand for the final statement of their chorale so as to 'drown everything, even the trumpets'.

Only one critic, it seems, was able to appreciate what it was that Mahler had attempted to achieve through his individual use of instrumental colour. One particular comment of his sums up the essential characteristics that came to typify the Mahler 'sound':

'This technical superiority easily leads him to choose rough sonorities to exaggerate expressions and sound effects'.

August Beer in the German newspaper<br>'Pester Lloyd'

Mahler was understandably upset by the work's failure, the more so since pressure of work at the opera had currently prevented him from losing himself in new projects. His unpredictable sense of humour did not desert him, however, as he related how, at the first performance, one elderly lady, sound asleep during the third movement, was rudely awakened by the cymbal crash 'attacca' into the finale and dropped all her belongings on the floor!

In January 1891, a dramatic turn for the worst took place at the opera when Beniczky resigned as Intendant and the one-armed Count Zichy took over. Mahler recognised an impasse when he saw one. Zichy was, after all, pledged to minimising his (Mahler's) powers of authority at the opera and would plainly stop at nothing to do just that. Refusing, however, to be pressurised into any premature move, Mahler devised a plan to play Zichy at his own game. Discreetly, he entered into fruitful negotiations with Bernhard Pollini at the Hamburg Opera and, with the firm offer of a contract there now secretly under his belt, he returned to Zichy with an apparent compromise. He (Mahler) would relinquish a number of his contractual rights in exchange for a new two-year contract (his original contract still had eight years to run) and compensation of 25,000 Gulden to be paid immediately upon termination. Just as Mahler had suspected he would, Zichy seized the bait and unhestitatingly offered him the stipulated compensation, thus effecting an automatic end to his contract.

With this unexpected but welcome windfall Mahler was able to purchase a spacious flat in Vienna for his remaining brothers and sisters. Zichy, meanwhile, smug in his apparent triumph, must have been furious when he learned of the Hamburg appointment. Not only could he have saved his company the sizeable redundancy payment but in the eyes of the public Mahler had now come to be regarded as something of a martyr. Budapest bade him farewell like a God with various tokens of gratitude: a gold baton, a laurel wreath in Hungary's national colours, and a vase inscribed with the words, 'To Gustav Mahler, artist of genius, from his Budapest admirers'.

Moreover, not all Zichy's nationalists had remained loyal to his witchhunt. Ferenz Erkel actually provided this epitaph in recognition of Mahler's directorship:

'This German Jew was the only man capable of transforming the hitherto polyglot Hungarian Opera into a unified national institution'.

# 6. Hamburg

'One cannot imagine how beautiful and animated this city is', Mahler wrote to his sister Justine on arriving in Hamburg. The date was March 26th 1891.

Bernhard Pollini, the theatre director, had temporarily placed his luxurious villa at the disposal of his 'star' arrival. Climate and surroundings were more than welcoming and Mahler's health appeared to be improving daily. At first glance, the diversity of repertoire and sheer range of Mahler's duties, both artistic and administrative, looked set to dispel any doubts he might have had that, for all its prestige and glamour, Hamburg would turn out to be a retrograde step after Budapest. Suffice it to say that his initial idealogy was not destined to last.

Hamburg was Germany's second city and the presence of Hans von Bülow and Bernhard Pollini at the helm of its opera house drew the eyes of Germany, indeed the world. Bernhard Pollini was probably the ablest and most unscrupulous impressario of his time. A sharp awareness of public taste, matched only by his obsession with box office success, eventually earned him the nickname of

*Opposite* Mahler, 1896.

*Right* Hamburg.

The State Theatre, Hamburg, where Mahler was director from 1891-1897.

'Monopollini'. Another ex-opera singer, he had begun his theatrical ventures in Russia with an Italian touring company, moving to Hamburg in 1874 with sizeable financial assets of his own and a head full of profitable ideas for the opera. His proposition was simply this: in return for two and a half per cent of the gross profits he would extensively re-structure the house to a new level of efficiency.

By the time Mahler arrived, Pollini's business cunning had already met with a considerable degree of commercial success. He had succeeded in drawing the biggest operatic names of the day to perform in Hamburg. Wisely, he had held fast to the prestige of Hans von Bülow as his musical director, despite violent disagreements between them over matters of policy and priority, and now, to cap it all, he had secured the services of the most closely watched conducting talent of that decade: Gustav Mahler. His plan was to nurture Mahler as von Bülow's successor.

Mahler, of course, soon became uneasy when he realised that Pollini's house policies were governed purely by commercial considerations. The roster of singers in Hamburg was indeed of the finest quality, but having just experienced and overcome the all-embracing 'star' system in Budapest, he was not about to welcome the prospect of having to contend with it all over again. Among the celebrated names that Pollini had contracted for regular appearances with the company were: Katharina Klafsky, principal soprano and a renowned 'Leonora' in Beethoven's *Fidelio*, tenors Max Alvary and Julius Lieban, and contralto, Ernestine Schumann-Heink. Pollini made it his business to travel extensively in search of new talent. His 'bonus' scheme for guest artists assured him the

50

cream of Europe's operatic circuit at all times, while his punishing schedules provided an enormously profitable turn-over of programmes: a different opera virtually every night of the week. During Mahler's first two months in Hamburg he conducted all of Wagner's major operas, Weber's *Die Freischütz* and *Euryanthe*, *Fidelio*, Mozart's *Don Giovanni* and *Die Zäuberflöte* and Mascagni's *Cavalleria Rusticana*. Extensive new repertoire, too, came his way over the next six years. Puccini's *Manon Lescaut*, Verdi's *Falstaff*, Humperdinck's *Hansel and Gretel* and Smetana's *Dalibor* and *The Bartered Bride*.

The age old problem with so prolific an output, though, was that it gave Mahler so very little time for thorough preparation. As we have seen already, nothing was more frustrating to him. Plainly Pollini was just not interested in the quality of theatre that he was producing. Stagecraft, lighting, costumes and scenery tended to be regarded as superfluous luxuries, so that for Mahler to even attempt implementing the successful amalgum of music and theatre that had

Bernhard Pollini, director of
The Hamburg Opera.

been his triumph in Budapest would have been foolhardy here. While Pollini remained, Hamburg was not, and never could be, a repertory ensemble in any real sense.

Under the circumstances, Mahler's achievements there were remarkable. That he succeeded in raising standards at all was yet another miracle of perseverance on his part. Musically, he was, as ever, ruthless in his pursuit of perfection. To combat the overloaded schedules he would call interminable rehearsals and from his scandalously under-paid musicians he continued to demand a level of nuance and refinement that, in fact, many instruments of the day (particularly wind) were simply incapable of producing.

Von Bülow was quickly impressed with Mahler's work – and he was a formidable man to impress. Icy, sarcastic and, as was fashionable, anti-semitic, he did not give of his admiration freely:

'Hamburg now has a new, first-class opera conductor, Gustav Mahler (a serious energetic Jew from Budapest), who, in my opinion, equals the greatest (Mottl, Richter etc.). Recently I heard "Siegfried" conducted by him . . . and felt deep admiration for the way in which – without a single orchestral rehearsal – he forced those rascals to dance to his tune'. (Hans von Bülow to his daughter, April 24th, 1891).

One irreconcilable area between them, however, and between Brahms and Mahler for that matter, was Mahler's own music: 'If this is music, then I know nothing of music', Bülow once exclaimed, and when Mahler played him the first movement of his Second Symphony on the piano, the old man remarked that it 'made "*Tristan and Isolde*" sound like a Haydn symphony . . . '.

It naturally depressed Mahler that men of von Bülow and Brahms' standing remained so unresponsive to his music. He once said: 'I could endure anything if only the future of my works was assured', and yet here, in theory, were men with the influence to ensure just that. In moments of despondency Mahler's thoughts would invariably turn to Anton Bruckner, his 'undiscovered' friend and mentor. One letter, written from Hamburg to his sister Justine, expressed what were perhaps his own worst fears:

'Received a touching letter from Bruckner which reveals the poor man's complete frustration. It really is hard to have to wait 70 years to be played. Unless the omens deceive, my fate will not be different from his'.

Twice in Hamburg Mahler gave performances of Bruckner's *Te Deum* to jubilant acclaim. In his own copy of the score he crossed out the words 'for Soli, Chorus, Organ and Orchestra' and wrote instead, 'For the tongues of heaven-blessed angels, chastened hearts and souls purified by fire'. Nothing, I think, better expresses the gratitude that Mahler felt towards Bruckner as a source of strength and inspiration. In so many ways they were kindred spirits: men of vision in a traditional, often hostile, environment. Only time would bring them acceptance.

One distinguished visitor to Hamburg during December 1891

was Tchaikovsky – there to finalise preparations for the German première of his opera *Eugene Onegin*. Mahler described him to Justine as 'an elderly gentleman, very likeable, with elegant manners, who seems quite rich and reminds me somehow of Mihalovics'. He was, it seems, less taken with the opera.

The première was set for January 19th, 1892, and Mahler had thus far been responsible for supervising rehearsals in readiness for the composer. At the final rehearsal Tchaikovsky himself presided, with some difficulty apparently, losing himself several times on account of changes in the recitative. Or so he maintained. That night he was guest of honour at the opera for a performance of *Tannhäuser* and was so impressed by Mahler's conducting that he decided then and there to entrust him with the opening night of *Onegin*. Mahler's subsequent comments on the opera make one wonder if this was something of a mixed blessing for him. On the other hand, he was already a firm admirer of the composer's work and the opera *Pique Dame* (The Queen of Spades) would later become not only a great personal favourite of his but one of his major triumphs in Vienna. *Onegin* was a moderate success. As usual it was hampered by paltry sets and costumes and little or no feeling for dramatic credibility; in the light of Pollini's policies, that went without saying. Nevertheless, the composer was well pleased with what Mahler had succeeded in achieving musically and the critics and public were kind, if not enthusiastic.

Peter Ilyich Tchaikovsky.

Tchaikovsky died two years later on November 6, 1893, and it was Mahler who conducted the memorial concert in Hamburg. One critic was 'unable to detect the slightest melodic invention' in the Fantasy Overture, *Romeo and Juliet*, which featured on that programme. Such astonishing critical insensibility was, alas, all too familiar to Mahler.

In the summer of 1892 Mahler made his first and only visit to London for a prestigious season of German opera at the Royal Opera House, Covent Garden, then under the directorship of Sir Augustus Harris. Centrepiece of the season was to be a complete cycle of Wagner's *Der Ring des Nibelungen* (performed in London only once before in 1882) and between them, Pollini and Harris had assembled an exciting line up of Germany's leading artists. The basic nucleus came from the Hamburg company, of course (Klafsky and Alvary for instance), but the addition of a few Bayreuth stars – Rosa Suchar and Theodor Reichmann among them – gave the ensemble its final touches of commercial distinction. To conduct the season, which was also to include performances of *Tristan und Isolde*, *Fidelio* and *Tannhäuser* (*Tristan* and *Fidelio* both scheduled to take place at the Theatre Royal, Drury Lane), Harris wanted Hans Richter, celebrated conductor of the Vienna State Opera and a popular visitor to London. Richter, however, was too

Programme for Mahler's visit to The Royal Opera House, Covent Garden, 9-16 July 1892.

heavily committed in Vienna at the time to accept, and Pollini shrewdly put forward Mahler knowing full well that his protégé's success in so auspicious a season was bound to reflect favourably on himself. 'Probably the most important conductor of his day' was how he presented his suggestion to Harris. Harris, of course, responded accordingly.

Shortly after his arrival in London, Herman Klein, critic of the *Sunday Times*, was invited to sit in on one of Mahler's *Tristan* rehearsals. He provided this revealing thumbnail sketch from his impressions:

'Mahler was now in his thirty-second year. He was rather short, of thin, spare build, with a dark complexion and small piercing eyes that stared at you with a not unkindly expression through large gold spectacles. I found him extraordinarily modest for a musician of his rare gifts and established reputation . . . I began to realise the remarkable magnetic power and technical mastery of his conducting. His men, whom he rehearsed first of all in sections, soon understood him without difficulty. Hence the unity of idea and expression existing between orchestra and singers that distinguished these performances of the '*Ring*' under Mahler as compared with any previously seen in London'.

Mahler conducted eighteen performances between 8th June and 23rd July. In some cases, London audiences, still subjected in the main to German or even Italian opera in English, were hearing these scores in their language of origin for the first time. The press were generally enthusiastic about Mahler's Wagner, but his reading of Beethoven's *Fidelio* apparently raised a few eyebrows – not least his, by all accounts, blisteringly theatrical delivery of the *Leonora No. 3* Overture which he now always inserted between the two scenes of Act Two. Among those meting out music criticism at the time was Bernard Shaw – generally more entertaining than constructive – and there were other would-be famous faces to be seen in the audiences, too. Henry Wood was an impressionable twenty-two, and one young composition student from the Royal College of Music was so moved by Mahler's *Tristan* that he remained sleepless for two nights afterwards. His name was Ralph Vaughan Williams.

The season was a revelation to the London public. Clearly they shared few, if any, of the critical reservations that one or two of the press had put forward: 'They overwhelm me with endless tokens of sympathy . . . a regular hurricane of applause', wrote Mahler to Arnold Berliner, an aquaintance of his in Hamburg. 'I've got to go before the curtain literally after every act – the whole house yells "Mahler" till I appear'.

The adulation of this or any other season, though, was still not enough to sustain Mahler through the prospect of increasingly arduous schedules in Hamburg. It worried him that the summer of 1892 had come and gone without his having so much as put pen to paper in composition. Success had brought him the means to buy some measure of time and freedom in which to practise his own creative pursuits. He now needed to apply these assets more efficiently. 'I conduct to live', he once said. 'I live to compose'.

1893 was a major step forward in this respect. He discovered Steinbach, a small village on the beautiful wooded lake of the Attersee. Here, amidst the scenic grandeur of the Salzkammergut, was the perfect setting, he thought, in which to set about a regular annual commitment to composition. During the summer, he and the family, accompanied by Natalie Bauer-Lechner (the source of so much revealing insight into Mahler's character on account of her scrupulous documentation over the years), took rooms in a one-

Natalie Bauer-Lechner, a close and devoted friend of Mahler's prior to his marriage in 1902.

Mahler's 'Hauschen' at Steinbach am Attersee where he worked on his second and third symphonies during the summers of 1893-1896.

storey inn just a few minutes walk from the village. Nearby, in a large open field leading down to the peninsula, plans were laid for the construction of a small work-hut or *hauschen* to be completed, it was hoped, in time for the following summer.

Thus began a rigorous summer routine. The day's work pattern was much the same. Mahler would rise early at around 6.30 and work through until lunch. Lunch was frugal and non-alcoholic in an attempt to discourage the migraines and digestive ills to which he was prone. The luxury of a cigar after eating was as much as he would allow himself in the way of indulgence. Justine would unwrap it for him in a kind of daily ritual. She maintained that, as she did so, the expression on his face alone was enough to reveal just how succesful the morning's work had been.

For the first time in his life, Mahler was actually experiencing what it was like to live the life of a composer. From the knowledge that at least three months of every year would now be given over exclusively to this end, he drew great satisfaction. Wryly, he once described himself as *der sommerkompanist*, 'the summer-composer'. As he later put it in a letter to the critic and composer, Max Marschalk:

'A man who is chained to the galleys of the theatre cannot manage to write as much music as the concert matadors of the day. He can only write on red-letter days. On these occasions all his emotional experiences concentrate themselves into one work. I am constitutionally unable to do anything but pour body and soul into each new work'.

The creative process itself was indeed a selfish business. Mahler related to nobody while he was working. The slightest disturbance was blown up out of all proportion. Even the very sounds of nature – the source of so much inspiration to him – were an intrusion into this enclosed world of productivity. Sister Justine would spend a good deal of her time erecting makeshift scarecrows or discreetly paying off local village musicians who came too close. Stray animals were driven off or locked up, and those which were noisy and edible tended to be bought and eaten – or so the story goes!

There were occasions, Mahler recalled, when he would sit at his desk unable to fathom exactly how the notes were finding their way on to the page. 'We do not compose: *we are composed*', he once said, and here was the proof. Music was an involuntary expression of his innermost soul driven by some intangible spiritual power beyond. Everyone and everything took second place.

'One is nothing but an instrument on which the universe plays. All those who live with me have had to learn this. At such times I don't belong to myself. I cannot be otherwise. . .the creator. . .must endure many hours of solitude and of absence during which he is lost in himself and entirely cut off from the outside world'.

During the three months intensive work of 1893, Mahler became deeply preoccupied with the mysteries of salvation and immortality; or, as he saw it, the object of life's toil and sorrow after death. 'Whence do we come? Whither does our road take us? Will the meaning of life be revealed by death? Such fundamental questions were laid down as the foundations for his mighty Second Symphony – later subtitled *The Resurrection*. His answers to them would all but turn the art of symphonic composition upside-down. Here was a vision of man's struggle for eternal salvation in the face of persistent doubts: the first really concrete exposé of his own God-fearing insecurities: 'You are battered to the ground with clubs and lifted to the heights on angels wings'.

The first movement was already virtually intact in the shape of his symphonic poem *Totenfeier*: an intense and stormy funeral march full of wild conflict and extreme contrast. The second and third movements were to inhabit worlds of Schubertian grace, albeit under the constant threat of restless undercurrents, and the fourth was to be the Wunderhorn song *Urlicht* for contralto, designed in effect as a spellbinding and ethereal prelude to the enormous fifth movement – a moment of almost childlike simplicity before the impending cataclysm.

The basic concept behind his huge choral finale was nothing less than a graphic and dramatic depiction of Judgment Day itself. In terms of sheer theatrical logistics alone, such a movement had never been attempted in symphonic music before: The opening bars, so strongly redolent of the Beethoven Ninth finale, burst in upon the stillness of the *Urlicht* like an agonising scream; offstage trumpets and horns sound ominously from afar; the 'Dies Irae', at first solemnly intoned in the lower brass, builds to a blaze of fanfares summoning the dead to arise from their graves and await judgment; an eerie silence – and then, unadorned terror as two shuddering percussion crescendos erupt into a grotesque and frenzied march. Panic is everywhere.

'The earth quakes, the graves burst open, and the dead arise and stream on in endless procession. The great and the little ones of the earth – kings and beggars, righteous and godless – all press on; the cry for mercy and forgiveness strikes fearfully on our ears. The wailing rises higher – our senses desert us; consciousness dies at the approach of the eternal spirit'.
(Original programme version of the second symphony,
as related by Mahler to Alma, 14th December, 1901)

Like any of the verbal or written descriptions that Mahler was sometimes grudgingly coaxed into providing for his music, these explicit programme notes for the second were quickly disowned as little more than a crutch for the unimaginative.

'They give only a superficial indication – all that any programme can do for a work – let alone this one, which is so much of a piece that it can no more be explained than the world itself. I'm quite sure if God were asked to draw up a programme of the world he had created, he could never do it'.
                                    (Mahler to Alma, Dresden, 15th December, 1901).

The work's final resolution eluded Mahler for some time. Just as the opening of the movement had borne a certain similarity to the opening of the Beethoven Ninth finale, so he was anxious to find a choral text which would express for him 'the glory of eternal redemption' just as Beethoven's use of Schiller's Ode to Joy had expressed universal brotherhood at the close of his Ninth.

Ironically, it was at the funeral of his colleague Hans von Bülow, who died in Cairo the following year, 1894, that the solution finally came to him. Ironical because Bülow's admiration for Mahler as a conductor had never extended to his music. At one key point in the funeral service, the choir sang a well-known choral ode by Friedrich Klopstock – *Aufersteh'n*. Its very first line: *Aufersteh'n, ja aufersteh'n* (To be resurrected, yes, to be resurrected) struck an immediate response in Mahler: 'everything was revealed clear and plain to my soul in a flash'.

The closing pages of the 'Resurrection' Symphony are among the most transcendentally beautiful that Mahler ever penned.

The hysteria has finally subsided leaving the air pure and motionless. From the distance once more, the 'last trump' sounds; above it, the lone song of a nightingale (solo flute) can be heard floating hypnotically on the rarified air. At last one can breathe again.

What follows now must rank as one of the most heart-stopping moments in the whole of symphonic literature. Unaccompanied, in barely a whisper, the chorus steal into the silence with Klopstock's resurrection hymn. Evolution is complete, redemption is finally at hand and, relentlessly, Mahler builds his massive forces into an accumulative blaze of rapturous affirmation: voices rise in ecstasy, bells chime, the augmented brass choir swells, and a vision of eternal life unfolds before our eyes, if but for a few moments of glowing certainty. In Mahler's words; 'An overwhelming love lightens our being. We know, and are'.

On the 29th June 1894, Mahler wrote from Steinbach to his friend Friedrich Löhr':

*Opposite* The magical entry of the chorus from the Fifth Movement of the Second Symphony, taken from the score in Mahler's own hand.

'This is to announce the auspicious birth of a strong, healthy last movement for the Second (Symphony). Father and child are doing as well as can be expected; the latter is not yet out of danger. It is to be baptised with the name 'Lux lucet in tenebris' (The light shineth in darkness). Friends are asked for their silent sympathy; all flowers are gratefully refused. Other gifts, however, will be accepted'.

59

The first three instrumental movements were performed in Berlin by the Berlin Philharmonic in March 1895, and on December 13th the score was given in full for the first time. Its dazzling impact on both audience and performers alike did not, predictably, extend to the critics. Violently divided they remained.

The very same summer that brought the birth of the second symphony saw, too, the final revisions to the First Symphony. Its third performance at the Weimar Festival on June 29th 1894, now bearing the subtitle *Titan*, was not more of an unqualified success than the previous two, except that instrumental in bringing about its inclusion in that particular programme, and responsible also for the supervision of rehearsals, was none other than Richard Strauss. Strauss was four years Mahler's junior, yet at 30 he had already achieved a status in the musical hierarchy that must have made Mahler deeply envious. *Don Juan, Macbeth, Tod und Verklärung* (Death and Transfiguration) and *Aus Italien* were already upon the scene and establishing themselves as standard repertoire. If only from a commercial point of view, his future was assured. Mahler never could understand Strauss' obsessional preoccupation with money. He would conduct anything and anywhere if the price was right and always under the false premise that one day he hoped to be rich enough to settle down and devote all his energies to composition. Secure in the knowledge that inspiration waits for no man, this was one philosophy which Mahler viewed with scepticism. It was a complete anathema to his own idealistic nature that Strauss was able to remain so cool in his approach to the tender art of creativity.

Richard Strauss at the time of his first meeting with Mahler.

Of Strauss' music itself, nobody, least of all Mahler, could deny the skill and brilliance that he displayed in his manipulation of the orchestra. Unlike Mahler though, he was quite prepared to pander to public whim whenever necessary and rarely did he plumb the depths of his own soul as Mahler did. In many respects his music was a reflection of his own showiest qualities.

Extraordinarily, the two men did manage to preserve a love-hate bond of sorts over the years. While paying a certain amount of lip-service to the younger man's success and status out of diplomacy, there is no doubt that Mahler did, nonetheless, greatly admire Strauss' technical facility – his acute ear for instrumental colour – just as Strauss remained curious, if to some extent patronising, of the Mahler enigma. Rarely can two artists of the same period have achieved such success and immortality from two such opposite standpoints.

Of all those in Mahler's life during this period, none was to be more significant than the 17-year old Jewish musician who arrived in Hamburg as coach and chorus master. Bruno Schlesinger, later known to the world as Bruno Walter, went on to provide us with some of the most illuminating of all Mahler memorabilia: all the more valuable, of course, for being seen through the eyes of a fellow conductor.

Mahler first came to Walter's attention by way of those largely scathing notices for the Weimar performance of his *Titan* symphony. Their extreme hostility fascinated him and he knew immediately that it was somehow imperative for him to meet the man behind this extraordinarily controversial music. Better still, to work alongside him. An interview with Pollini was subsequently arranged and he was duly appointed as the new *Korrepetitor*.

Walter later described his first meeting with Mahler:

I immediately recognised him when I saw a lean, fidgety short man with an unusually high, straight brow, long, jet-black hair, deeply penetrating bespectacled eyes, and a characteristically 'spiritual' mouth. Pollini introduced us, and a brief conversation took place. Later on, Mahler's friendly and slightly amused account of it was to be laughingly repeated to me by his sisters. "So you are the new coach", Mahler said. "Do you play the piano well?" "Excellently", I replied, because any false modesty seemed unworthy of a great man. "Are you a good sight reader?" Mahler then asked. "Oh yes, very good", I said again truthfully. "And do you know the regular repertoire operas?" "I know them all quite well", I replied, with such self-confidence that Mahler burst out laughing, patted me kindly on the back, and concluded the conversation by saying, "Well, well . . . that certainly sounds most promising!" '

(Bruno Walter, Theme and Variations).

The young Bruno Walter, life-long friend and devotee of Mahler's music.

Walter's confidence there certainly belied his total lack of experience, but Mahler was quick to recognise his natural abilities and encourage him in every way possible. Their working relationship very soon blossomed into something much more personal. Though almost half Mahler's age, and so very junior in status, Walter took great stimulation from the fact that no barriers appeared to exist between them. They spent many happy social hours discussing the likes of Schopenhauer, Dostoyevsky and Nietzsche or playing four-handed piano works by Schubert, Mozart, Schumann or Dvorak. Intellectually, there was nothing, it seems, that Mahler was unwilling to share with his young disciple:

'I felt as if a higher realm had opened up to me – Mahler, in looks and behaviour, struck me as a genius, a demon; life itself had suddenly become romantic. I cannot better describe the elemental power of Mahler's personality than by saying that its irresistible effect on a young musician was to produce in him . . . an entirely new attitude to life'.

Not that Walter was blind to his hero's quirks:

61

'I was fascinated to observe how the same intensity, the same spiritual tenseness that had previously filled his rehearsing was now manifested in his conversation. The vehemence with which he objected when I said something that was unsatisfactory to him . . . his sudden submersion into pensive silence, the kind glance with which he would receive an understanding word on my part, an unexpected, convulsive expression of secret sorrow and, added to all this, the strange irregularity of his walk: his stamping of the feet, sudden halting, rushing ahead again – everything confirmed and strengthened the impression of demoniac obsession'.

Walter was with the Mahlers and Natalie Bauer-Lechner in Steinbach during the summer of 1895: a period of astonishing creative accomplishment when Mahler's inspiration appeared to go to the very heart of existence. Not since childhood had he craved so desperately for the absolution and refuge of his surroundings. Completion of the mighty Second Symphony, to say nothing of his crippling responsibilities in Hamburg now that von Bülow was dead, had thoroughly sapped his reserves of strength. Worst of all, his favourite brother Otto had finally committed suicide in February of that year in spite of all Mahler's efforts to help and encourage him. Mahler always maintained that Otto had the potential to be a greater musician than he. It distressed him deeply that he had proved so hopelessly inadequate to the challenge.

The Salzkammergut had rarely appeared quite so overwhelming in its majesty as it did that summer. Mahler walked and climbed endlessly. It was as if he were being drawn, mentally and physically, into those forbidding alpine vistas while, simultaneously, visions of the great god Dionysus, of Pan, of every elemental force in nature seemed to converge on him in 'one gigantic hymn to the glory of every aspect of creation'. That, it seems, is precisely how his gargantuan Third Symphony came to be conceived and those were the words he initially used to describe it on returning to Hamburg that autumn. In the broadest sense, the Third brought together the three principal sources of his inspiration – Nature, Man and God – in one all-embracing celebration; 'of such magnitude' he later wrote to Anna von Mildenburg, 'that it mirrors the whole world – one is so, to speak, an instrument played on by the universe . . . In my symphony the whole of nature finds a voice'.

To be sure, Mahler never again delved into the miracle of nature to such an exhaustive degree. Bruno Walter recalls how they were strolling in the mountains one day when Mahler suddenly turned on him and said: 'No need to look up there – I've composed all that already'. And from Natalie Bauer-Lechner came a similar story when she and Mahler were walking, on another occasion, amidst what could only be described as a medley of village sounds: 'Do you hear it?' Mahler exclaimed, 'That's polyphony. That's where I got it from'. Such incidents crystalise the character of this music.

*Opposite* The inn at Steinbach in the magnificent Salzkammergut.

The Third absorbed Mahler throughout 1895 and 1896, the bulk of the groundwork being completed during that first summer. For a while he considered calling it a symphonic poem just as he had originally done with the First. Until, that is, he stopped short and asked himself a couple of very leading questions – What is a symphony? When is a symphony still a symphony?: 'The term "symphony" – to me this means creating a world with all the technical means available. The constantly new and changing content determines its own form'. Indeed, Mahler was inescapably at the very forefront of what was to be a major upheaval of symphonic form. Berlioz had already pushed back the boundaries significantly with his *Symphonie Fantastique* (a work that Mahler was later to adopt into his conducting repertoire). Mahler's extravagant new opus would take the process one stage further.

Originally he planned to subtitle the six movements (or seven as it was then) under a general overall heading. 'The Gay Science' after Nietzsche, was one favoured possibility. Eventually, though, just as had been the case with his first and second symphonies, the need for explanation regressed as musical ideas developed. Mahler's attitude to programme music was clearly ambivalent. On the one hand descriptive elements were an inspiration to him, and on the other, he wanted only to cut the umbilical cord and allow the music to speak for itself. In his study *The Wunderhorn Years*, musicologist Donald Mitchell writes:

'. . . the programme in a very vital sense generated the work, and the work was then launched with at least enough of the programmatic scaffolding still visible to serve as an aid to the comprehension of the music by its first audience. . . the enormous importance of the dramatic programme for the early symphonies cannot be gainsaid: the symphonies *are* the programmes, embodied and transcended, it is true, but unthinkable without them . . .'.

In the case of the third symphony, the subtitles of the final version still find their way on to our concert programmes despite Mahler's insistence to the contrary. In the final draft, the movements were laid out as follows:

1. Summer marches in.
2. What the flowers in the meadow tell me.
3. What the animals in the forest tell me (featuring an evocative off-stage solo for posthorn in B flat).
4. What night tells me (of man): a setting for contralto of words by Nietzsche expressing man's longings and desperate loneliness.
5. What the morning bells tell me (of Angels): for contralto, boys and women's choirs.

6. What love tells me ('Above all, Eternal Love spins a web of light like rays of sun converging to a single burning point').

A seventh movement 'What the child tells me', which was to utilise his early Wunderhorn song *Das Himmlische Leben* (Life in Heaven), was wisely dropped from the plan of the Third Symphony and placed instead as the final movement of his Fourth. To have attempted to follow the surpassing Adagio that stands now at the apex of this extraordinary work would have been inconceivable. It remains one of Mahler's most heartfelt inspirations: his first great symphonic Adagio cast in a truly Brucknerian mould of devout spiritual calm, and culminating in a radiant coda glorifying the loftiest ideals in all creation.

Mahler later confided: 'I could almost call the movement "What God tells me". And truly, in the sense that God can only be understood as love. And so my work . . . begins with inanimate nature and ascends to the love of God'.

His astounding first movement 'Summer marches in' was conceived, if you like, as the elaborate portal through which one would gain access to the unfolding miracle beyond. Lengthy (about 35 minutes) and unorthodox in construction (though hardly formless and sprawling as is frequently maintained) it has remained the most controversial and – in terms of orchestral colour – the most daringly innovative of the symphony's eventual six movements.

Mahler saw it as depicting the banishment of winter, 'the victorious appearance of Helios and the miracle of spring thanks to which all things live, breathe, flower, sing and ripen', and ultimately the tumultuous arrival of summer itself, conceived as 'a conqueror advancing amidst all that grows and blooms'. He envisaged the brazen procession of Dionysus coursing in upon wintry landscapes; a cacophony of rabble-rousing military bands and raucous high spirits. The movement, he said, would take on 'a humorous, even baroque style'.

In the event, his prodigiously individual gift for orchestral tone-painting rarely found so flamboyant an outlet. From the eight unison horns that thunder out the opening march tune through the shuddering bass frequencies and elephantine trombone solos of winter's primeval rumblings to the arrival of the noisy parade itself, his rich canvas encompasses myriad vivid extremes in colour and mood. By even Mahler's standards, the exultant coda of the movement is a most fantastic piece of orchestral virtuosity: a veritable erruption of rollocking horns, wild trumpet calls and pounding percussion.

Of those who were with Mahler during the period of the Third Symphony's germination, only Bruno Walter was privileged enough to penetrate the composer's enclosed world. Few ever shared that privilege.

'I was overwhelmed by the sense his playing conveyed, of the fire and rapture in which the work was conceived. Only now, through his music, did I really understand him; his entire being seemed to breathe a mysterious rapport with nature. I had faintly sensed the elemental intensity of this before, while now I experienced it directly through the sound language of his symphonic world dream'.

(Walter, 'Theme and Variations').

Back in Hamburg there were further crises. During Mahler's summer recess in 1895, principal soprano Katharina Klafsky, whose husband Otto Lohse was second conductor with the company, broke contract and disappeared with him to America. Pollini invited Walter to take over Lohse's position and, as a replacement for Klafsky, engaged a captivating and immensely talented dramatic soprano barely 23 years old. Her name was Anna von Mildenburg and, like Rosa Papier the Bayreuth star who recommended her, she was destined to become one of the great singing legends of the age. Moreover, she would draw Mahler into the longest and most turbulent love affair of his life, riding the crest of success with him right through to his celebrated Vienna regime.

Soprano, Anna von Mildenburg.

Her artistic future was sealed the minute that Mahler set eyes upon her.

Pollini's somewhat out-dated concept of the true dramatic soprano meant that he had hitherto regarded her slim figure as a distinct disadvantage where the rigours of the great Wagnerian roles were concerned. At one point he even suggested that she put on weight as a means of conserving energy! Mahler, on the other hand, saw in her visual credibility and fine voice the beginnings of a new era in the dramatic refinement of opera production. She represented another breed of operatic artist altogether and he was determined to nurture her talent to his own ends.

Mildenburg was understandably apprehensive about her initial encounters with the maestro. His tyrannical reputation had been painted very black in some quarters and she was afraid that he might simply intimidate her. On the contrary, though, the care and expertise that he lavished upon their work together soon dispelled any of her doubts. They quickly found themselves swept away on a tide of mutual admiration. He inspired her to new levels of confidence while she reciprocated by hanging on to his every word. Like Alma after her, Anna was to some extent prepared to succumb to the supreme ego and self-concern that went hand in hand with Mahler's genius. Before long, however, her own tempestuous, hypersensitive nature began to create obstacles in their personal relationship.

'I have already told you that I am at work on a great composition (the Third Symphony). Can't you understand how that takes up all of a man?' came one rebuke to her excessive demands.

Sister Justine, meanwhile, had developed a curious jealousy towards this rival for her brother's affections and the Hamburg gossips were, of course, buzzing with the scandal of the liaison.

No summer composition took place in 1897. Mahler had begun to find it impossible operating within the confines of Pollini's rigidly out-dated regime in Hamburg. Relations between the two men had progressively worsened since Von Bülow's death, and besides, Mahler's sights were now firmly fixed on higher ideals: namely Vienna. His resignation was tendered early in the year and in March he set off on his first international concert tour – a variably successful sojourn which took in Budapest, Moscow and Munich with a brief stop in Berlin to hear another rising young conductor, one Felix Weingartner, direct three movements of his Third Symphony.

Penetration of the musical strongholds in Berlin, Dresden, Munich (where Richard Strauss was now installed as chief conductor) and, of course, Vienna was virtually impossible for a non-Catholic, let alone a Jew. Mahler even enlisted the help of Brahms whom he had visited on a couple of occasions the previous year in Vienna and the summer resort of Bad Ischl, close to Steinbach; but to no avail. It was an unwritten law now that prestigious Court positions such as these were available only to Catholics. No other choice was open to him. If becoming a Catholic could ensure his passage to Vienna, then a Catholic he would become. As far as his own religion was concerned, he could regard himself without conscience as strictly unorthodox, and since generally his religious beliefs might best have been described as agnostic or even aesthetic – which would account for his fascination with the ritualistic elements in Catholic mysticism – it was a change that he could justify without too much soul-searching or guilt.

Rumours very soon spread through Vienna that his appointment was imminent. Joseph von Bezecny, the Intendant there, had endeavoured to underplay the details of what he knew was likely to be a controversial choice, but his intentions had already leaked out and the opposition, led by Principal Conductor, Hans Richter and second Conductor, Nepomuk Fuchs, sprang into action. They found a staunch supporter in Cosima Wagner who made no secret of her anti-semitic beliefs. Why else would the supreme Wagner interpreter of his day never have been invited to conduct at Bayreuth.

Bezecny was determined to capture Mahler. He, like others before him, realised all too well that only someone with Mahler's fanatical up-to-the-minute ideas and unswerving ideals could hope to pull the opera from its mortifying complacency. He realised too, of course, that the Viennese 'guardians of tradition' were unlikely to yield to change without a fight. For better or worse, Vienna still set iself up as a musical environment of dignity, respectability and unstinting conservatism: an environment where age still signified wisdom and youth was always suspect.

'Suppose I did come to Vienna. With my attitude to things, what would happen to me there? The first time I tried to impose my interpretation of a Beethoven symphony upon the celebrated Philharmonic, trained by doughty Hans (Richter), the most hateful battle would ensue . . . I should bring a storm around my head whenever I departed from routine to make some contribution of my own'.

Mahler to Friedrich Löhr, 1894.

In spite of all, though, the appointment did go ahead and on May 1st Mahler was engaged as Kapellmeister. In a letter to Arnold Berliner shortly after his installation, he once again reiterated his apprehension. This time, however, his uncertainty was coloured with more than just a hint of characteristic determination:

Hans Richter.

For the time being, the summons to Vienna has brought me only unprecedented disturbance and the anticipation of battles to come. Whether it is the right place for me time alone can tell. In any case I must steel myself for a year's violent hostility on the part of those who either will not or cannot co-operate. (The two things usually go together). Hans Richter, in particular, is reported to be doing his level best to raise hell against me . . . But I am going back to my own country, and I shall put an end to my wandering in this life.

Within a year Vienna began to follow him. His progress was meteoric. On July 13th he was appointed deputy director to Wilhelm Jahn, Director of the Court Opera since 1881, and on October 8th the annoucement was made that he was to become Principal Conductor and Director with almost unlimited powers and more financial security than he had previously thought possible. At the age of 37, he was finally home: Vienna.

There could be no more compromises. For the Imperial Opera a golden reformation was within grasp, and for Mahler it was the realisation of a dream that he should be there at its inception:

'As a man I am willing to make every possible concession', he said, 'but as a musician I make none. Other opera directors look after themselves and wear out the theatre. I wear myself out and look after the theatre'.

# 7. *Vienna I*

Vienna – the city of Gluck, Haydn, Mozart, Beethoven, Schubert and Brahms; the city with an almost traditional reputation for reviling its great men while they lived and 'canonising them when they were dead', as musicologist Michael Kennedy once put it. Vienna was still very much the elegant capital of central Europe in the latter part of the 19th Century; a cosmopolitan mix of races and cultures: Slavs, French, Germans, Hungarians, Spaniards. Beneath its sugar-coated hospitality and courtesy, though, were harboured unseen decadence and inter-racial hatred. Its pavement coffee houses, for instance, where it was possible to personalise a regular table and have one's mail and papers delivered daily, had gradually become – behind the friendly charm – breeding grounds for all the current scandal and gossip-column fodder. As Director of the city's great cultural institution, the Opera, Mahler was inevitably a prime target for the sensation-mongers. His was the name on everyone's lips. Nothing he did, be it private or public, true or false, was likely to escape circulation. Nor was any outward change of religion on his part going to deter the ever-expanding anti-semite movement from using him as a scapegoat. Every day their underhand activities grew to smell more ominously like forerunners of the Nazi party.

The Jewish presence in Vienna played an essential part in the city's life, both on a cultural and business footing. Without its patronage Vienna's artistic functions would very soon have dropped to a level of provincial mediocrity. Perhaps this is precisely what the conservative die-hards had hoped would happen. They were, after all, quite content to escape forevermore into the frothy operettas of Johann Strauss and Lehar rather than confront the harsh realities of more progressive voices: composers like Arnold Schoenberg, Alban Berg and Anton von Webern, the revolutionary trio poised shortly to usher in a major new musical age; painters like Gustav Klimt and Egon Schiele and writers like Hofmannsthal and Schnitzler.

Vienna was at the crossroads between new and old ideals. Progress was at last beginning to reflect in every walk of life and, amongst those with the influence to bring about radical change,

*Opposite* Mahler, 1907.

71

*Top* The Imperial Court Opera House, Vienna. *Below – small inset* A Vienna street cafe.

Mahler now saw clearly how his key position in the artistic life of the capital could very easily tip the balance.

The Imperial Opera itself – the Hofoperntheater – was built between 1861 and 1869 at very much the same time and along very much the same lines as the Paris Opera. Set in the *Ringstrasse* – that magnificent horseshoe-curved civic heart of Vienna, site of the ancient ramparts and one of Emperor Franz Joseph's most cherished projects – it's neo-renaissance grandeur, elaborate ornamentations and superb acoustics were a triumph for architects August von Siccardsburg and Eduard van der Null.

The aforementioned Hans Richter – musical director at the time of Mahler's arrival – was a much revered pillar of the establishment: protégé of Wagner (hence the bond with Cosima), trustee of several Bayreuth premières, and a musician immoveably grounded in classical traditions. His relationship with Mahler was initially very cautious (the arrival of one twenty years his junior with all sorts of outlandish ideas understandably posed something of a threat) though, to be fair, as time went on he at least came round to acknowledging Mahler's far-reaching talents even if he did not directly approve in principle. As fortune would have it, Mahler's great advocate from the very start was Prince Montenuovo, the Emperor's Lord Chamberlain of the Household. Once his appointment as Principal Conductor and Director was confirmed, there was no-one else to whom he was directly answerable.

If the early days of Mahler's directorship in Vienna were turbulent, to say the least, his debut there on May 11th 1897, was certainly no indication. This was the first and perhaps the only time when Vienna, press and public alike, raised its voice to him in

Prince Montenuovo.

unanimous acclaim. The opera was *Lohengrin* and the performance, which was intended as something of a trial baptism for the new Kappelmeister, was a sensation. Rarely had the house experienced enthusiasm of this order. Natalie Bauer-Lechner recalls the hum of expectation in the air and the sporadic bursts of applause each time Mahler's tempi departed from accepted 'normality'. Even Vienna's most carping critics – and Mahler would come to experience the sting of their words in due course – for once bowed to his original talent:

Last night, on which Wagner's *Lohengrin* was given . . . evoked special interest through the presence of the newly acquired conductor Gustav Mahler in his first conducting appearance. Herr Mahler is of small, slender, energetic figure, with sharp, intelligent features . . . As the looks, so the conductor, full of energy and fine understanding. He belongs to the younger school of conducting, which, in contrast to the statuesque presence of the older conductors, has developed a livelier mimicry. Those younger ones speak with arms and hands, with twists of the entire body . . . Through such exterior means, which fully attained spiritual character, Herr Mahler conducted *Lohengrin*. With great understanding did he enter the dream world of the Prelude; only at the high point of the composition, when the brass enters with all its weight, did he grip the entire orchestra with quick, energetic transformation, his baton, swordlike, attacking the trombones. The result was magic. In the richly dramatic first act . . . Mahler exercised his conductor's art fully. His presence was everywhere. He stood in living relationship to orchestra, choir, individuals. Nobody missed his cues. Conductor Mahler found full appreciation from the public. After the prelude he had to bow repeatedly to the house, and loud shouts greeted the new man. Herr Mahler is not only an excellent conductor but also a splendid director . . . he is surely the right man for the present situation. One could not support the ailing director of the opera (Herr Jahn) more gently yet more realistically than by placing at his side such an artist. Herr Mahler will act as artistic leaven if we let him assert himself'.

Ludwig Speidel, 'Wiener Fremdenblatt' (12th May 1897)

Herr Mahler was, of course, soon given ample rein to assert himself, but would that critical reaction had remained this constructive. As it was, it hindered his progress at almost every turn.

Once in command of the crucial directorship, every aspect of production in Vienna came strictly under Mahler's personal supervision. Early reforms were quick to bite. Ruthlessly he dispensed with all out-moded ideas and sloppy habits. Latecomers would not be admitted until the end of an act, the houselights would be lowered before the curtain rose, and Wagner operas would be given complete without the savage mutilations that were so often imposed as a concession to non-musical opera-goers'

73

*Top* Otto Boehler's silhouettes of Mahler conducting in Vienna *Bottom* Selma Kurz.

powers of endurance. Strict rehearsal discipline was to apply to all strata of the company from chorus to the most illustrious of the principals. No lame excuses for absenteeism would be tolerated any longer and orchestral members would now be forbidden to exercise that age-old custom of sending deputies to rehearsals or performances while they busied themselves with lucrative freelance work.

As originator of the ensemble theory – a problem that many opera companies still find themselves grappling with today – Mahler's first sizeable task in Vienna was to bring about re-structuring of the company just as he had done in Budapest. No more jet-setting superstars stepping blithely into unfamiliar productions decked out in inappropriate costumes of their own and armed with a selection of spurious top notes and unwritten cadenzas (a custom which was particularly afflicting Mozart's operas). Great singers did not necessarily make a great company and Mahler's prime aim once again was to assemble a group of talented artists who were prepared to make some sort of long-term commitment to Vienna and cultivate a positive house-style.

Many of the existing company stalwarts had to go, of course. In virtually every case they had outlived their usefulness vocally and

*Top* Leo Slezak.
*Bottom* Erik Schmedes.

were no longer capable of matching Mahler's exacting standards. Their departures were, in the main, voluntary – for they found the maestro overpowering and excessively rude anyway – but the older sector of the Viennese audiences were predictably outraged. A number of their familiar 'favourites' were being put out to graze, as it were, only to be replaced – as they saw it – by an influx of precocious unknowns. Characteristically, all Mahler's soloists were painstakingly hand-picked. He would frequently engage fresh and inexperienced young artists if he recognised those vital sparks of potential. Not every gamble paid off, of course, but at least he was quick to admit a misjudgment even if some of his critics were not. Generally, he was more inclined to favour outstanding acting ability and an adequate voice than vocal perfection and an indifferent stage presence. When the two came together – as they had in the case of Anna von Mildenberg – he then had the means with which to create theatrical magic. And Vienna had been deprived of that for far too long.

It was a measure of Mahler's artistic courage and integrity that Anna von Mildenburg numbered amongst his principal sopranos in Vienna. Ever since the break-up of their disastrous affair, the gossip-mongers had been lying in wait. Her engagement in Vienna gave them every opportunity to re-open the scandal and again question his motives for employing her; but Mahler was unperturbed. His professional pride made it impossible for him to overlook her exceptional qualities as an artist. She was unique of her kind and only that was really important.

Other names appearing on the roster, in addition to Mildenburg, included: Marie Gutheil-Schoder, Erich Schmedes, Leo Slezak, Leopold Demuth, Friedrich Weidmann, Richard Mayr and Selma Kurz, possessor of what became known as the famous 'Selma trill'. Kurz conquered Vienna and Mahler virtually overnight with the beauty and agility of her voice. Twice she sang songs from his *Lieder Eines Fahrenden Gesellen* and each time, the matchless control of her pianissimo legato singing and 'the incomparable softness' of her personality, amazed and captivated him. She was also very beautiful. Not surprisingly a short-lived flirtation did ensue, except that this time Mahler proceeded with caution, no doubt in an attempt to avoid a repetition of the Mildenberg saga.

He often spoke quite openly of his inability to resist the lure of an outstanding musical talent allied to a beautiful woman. Conversely, though, he was just as readily repelled by any shortcomings relating to his very precious art:

'If a woman of whom I was attracted sang a single false note or un-musical phrase, all my affection for her would vanish instantly, and might even turn to hatred'.

75

Marie Gutheil-Schoder.

Therein lies the key, perhaps, to all Mahler's encounters with the opposite sex. It is dubious that any of his so-called 'affairs' were, in fact, motivated by sex at all but by more aesthetic romantic emotions. Music was still the one sure way into his affections, or rather, infatuations.

Not all the 'old brigade' in the Vienna company fled in fear and discontent at Mahler's controversial new ways. There were some, like Theodor Reichmann – a great 'Hans Sachs' and 'Wotan' – who were big enough to acknowledge his worth. Reichmann, who privately called Mahler 'the Jewish monkey' on account of the way he would leap from the rostrum and scurry through the double basses on to the stage during rehearsal, wrote in his diary on one occasion:

'The inspiration that radiates from this little man is fantastic. He makes you give more than you ever had'.

Of the newer company, many of whom were destined for great careers under Mahler's scrupulous guidance, tenors Erik Schmedes and Leo Slezak were wonderfully larger-than-life characters. Schmedes, with a weakness for the tavern, would often find himself personally escorted from his chosen watering hole by an extremely angry Mahler urgently requiring his presence at rehearsal. Remonstrations that he had sung the part before and knew it well were naturally met with deaf indifference. Yet, of Mahler, Schmedes unequivocally said:

'This is a stage manager and a conductor in whom the singer can have absolute confidence. I do not look at him when he is conducting, but the feeling that he is conducting sustains the singer and protects him from all the pitfalls, Mahler is a strict critic . . . so you can be all the more pleased by his praise'.

Leo Slezak was, by all account, the life and soul of any party: a rotund giant of a man with a superb Heldentenor voice that ranged effortlessly from Mozart to Wagner. Of the many superb anecdotes attributed to him, one in particular remains a classic. During a performance of *Lohengrin*, the swan pulling the boat for Lohengrin's final departure prematurely moved off before Slezak could even set foot on it. 'Sotto voce', he was heard to mutter: 'When does the next swan leave?'.

Of all the changes that Mahler implemented during his incumbency in Vienna, perhaps the most far-reaching were concerned with visual and dramatic presentation. The Imperial Opera offered unparalleled facilities in terms of what could be achieved on a technical level yet its resources had remained largely untapped on account of absurd inbred resistance to new ideas.

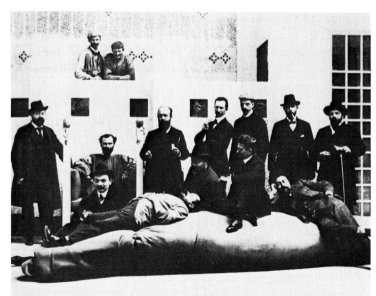

*Left* Members of the Vienna seccession preparing for their 14th exhibition, 1902.
*Right* The exhibition building of the Vienna seccession designed by Joseph Maria Olbrich and opened in 1898.

Resistance or no, Mahler again made his intentions plain from the start: 'Existing decors and costumes should go to the devil!'.

Certain structural modifications of his own were first made to the theatre to enable his campaign of reform to get underway. The orchestra pit itself was lowered to overcome light-spill problems, a telephone was installed to effect quicker communication with the stage in rehearsal and, during performance, a light-cue system was introduced to inform Mahler when the curtain was ready to rise lest some unsuspecting stage hand be caught putting the finishing touches to a lengthy scene change. Such refinements would be considered indispensible nowadays, yet Vienna and most houses of the period, however sophisticated, had long operated without them.

Mahler's principal ally in bringing about his presentation revolution at the Imperial Opera was one, Alfred Roller. Roller, a theatre designer and close friend of the Schindler family (into which Mahler was to marry) was himself part of a newly formed anti-establishment art organisation, aptly named 'The Secession', whose aim it was to voice artistic alternatives in the face of stagnating traditions. Painters Gustav Klimt, Egon Schiele, Oscar Kokoschka, Carl Moll (founder member and Alma Schindler's stepfather), Kolo Moser and Emil Orlik (who painted Mahler), sculptor Max Klinger and architects Otto Wagner and Adolf Löhse were at the forefront of its membership. Not surprisingly, Mahler was instinctively drawn by their progressive doctrines. For him they symbolised a major revival in Vienna's, indeed Europe's, visual standards: 'the great Viennese design revival', as he saw it, in which the operatic theatre could also play a significant part.

It didn't take long for the Secession's ornate influences to start permeating the whole environment. Clothes, furniture and houses

Alfred Roller.

were as susceptible to the advent of 'Art Nouveau' as the arts themselves, and by 1902, the year of the first great Secession Exhibition in Vienna, the new wave was spreading far and wide.

Mahler first met Alfred Roller at a party given by some of his friends. They had no sooner made each other's acquaintance when Roller began an earnest discourse upon the glories of Wagner's *Tristan und Isolde* and its trivialisation at the hands of the Imperial Opera's insipid staging. Few topics could have aroused feelings of such instant accord in Mahler. That particular production was already earmarked in his efforts to rid the house of the kind of crude stage 'realism' that was giving opera a bad name. For *Tristan und Isolde*, with its heightened passions and multi-faceted emotions, he had in mind an expressionistic visual approach such as had been introduced so triumphantly into his Budapest work. Roller more than shared his ideals.

A meeting was set up for the following day in Mahler's office at the opera house and there Roller elaborated upon his ideas for a completely new *Tristan* staging. After hearing what he had to say, Mahler was more convinced than ever that here was a man whose fertile imagination and uncompromising dedication coincided entirely with his own. It was Roller's first stage commission. The risks involved for Mahler were considerable. Nevertheless, this was an opportunity he could simply not afford to pass over. Roller was assigned the *Tristan* designs and a remarkable theatrical collaboration began.

*Tristan und Isolde* – the first performance of the opera to be given in Vienna without cuts – opened on 21st February 1903 to mark the 20th anniversary of Wagner's death. It was a sensation: bewildering to some, but a sensation nonetheless.

Predictably, the more rebellious press made capital out of its visual abstraction:

'We may betray to the curious who were unable to secure entry to the sold-out house that the first act is orange-yellow, the second mauve and the third dough-coloured. Friends of the Secession will be pleased to see Tristan and Isolde wandering amid strangely impressionistic landscapes. One thing should be made clear from the outset: of the spirit of Wagner – despite many artistic details, including for example Herr Schmedes' new nose – there was precious little to be seen . . .'
Hans Liebstöckl, 'Reichswehr', 22nd February 1903.

Roller's maxim was 'space, not pictures'. Utilising a symbolic interplay of light and scenic shapes geared towards a new-found simplicity, his aim was to fire the imagination, not dictate to it.

As for Mahler's musical contribution, Erwin Stein described his *Tristan* as 'feverish and even delirious . . . unrelieved, yearning

78

white-hot passion and violent suffering . . . the climaxes were shattering indeed'.

Erik Schmedes was 'Tristan' and Anna von Mildenburg was 'Isolde'. Hers was, by all accounts, a great tragic performance – perhaps the performance of her career.

Roller now became Vienna's permanent stage designer and in keeping with Mahler's belief that his duty, as director of the opera, was to guide public taste, not pander to it, their collaboration produced some of the period's most controversial, but memorable, operatic productions: a *Ring* cycle which at last rid the stage of superfluous clutter and attempted to plumb something of the work's metaphysical mystery; a legendary Beethoven *Fidelio* in 1904 with Mildenburg an unforgettable Leonora; Gluck's *Iphigenie en Aulide* which Mahler regarded as their finest achievement; a magical, kaleidoscopic *Der Freischütz*, and in 1905 their celebrated *Don Giovanni* in which Roller's famous 'towers' appeared for the first time. These were moveable, pylon-like structures which served, scenically, as all things to all situations and revolutionised fast and efficient scene changing.

Perhaps the words which still best convey the magnitude of Mahler and Roller's achievement during their extraordinary period of re-vitalisation in Vienna are those which appeared in *Neue Freie Presse* on 25th January 1905 – the occasion of their new *Das Rheingold* production which in turn launched their revelatory collaboration on Wagner's *Ring*. Julius Korngold (successor to Vienna's most eminent critic Eduard Hanslick and one of Mahler's staunchest supporters) wrote thus:

'But the most beautiful tales in this new production are told by the lights. They swathe the gods in brilliance and serenity; they leave them wallowing in murky mists. The movement on stage is frozen, as it were, into a series of pictures which are then, however, invested with a truly inner movement by the magical changes of lighting . . . The final subtle communion between stage and music is established in Mahler's art. It is he who gives light to the orchestra. The element of tone-painting, which in *Rheingold* predominates over emotional expression, is completely fused with the paintings on stage'.

During his epoch-making decade at the Imperial Opera, Mahler conducted over one thousand performances: one quarter of them Wagner. Mozart, Beethoven, Puccini, Smetana, Massenet, Tchaikovsky, R. Strauss, Charpentier, Gluck, Pfitzner, Giordano and Weber were among the other composers who featured most regularly. He championed Tchaikovsky's *Queen of Spades* along, of course, with *Eugene Onegin* and his last completed, one-act opera *Iolanta* which he premièred. Smetana's *Dalibor* was another major Mahler discovery, as were Puccini's *La Boheme*, Giordano's *Fedora*,

Charpentier's *Louise* and Offenbach's *Tales of Hoffman*. On the lighter side, Johann Strauss' *Die Fledermaus*, so much a part of Viennese heritage, was fortunately a particular favourite with Mahler (89 times he gave it in Vienna) and on New Year's Eve he would conduct a special performance in aid of the staff pension fund with some of the company's most illustrious stars singing in the chorus and real champagne in the glasses.

'He lived in everything and everything lived in him', wrote Bruno Walter summing up his genius as an opera conductor.

And no matter how foreign a sentiment might be to him, how contrary to his character, his imagination would enable him to place himself inside the most opposite person and in the strangest of situations. Thus, Mahler's heart was on stage when he sat at the desk. He conducted or, rather, he produced the music in accordance with the drama.

Mahler had succeeded, then, where most others would surely have failed. In the face of obstructive opposition he was yet again master of his own conditions. Prince Montenuovo lavished praise upon him at every opportunity and the general mass of the musical public, to say nothing of the more constructive critics, fell ever more willingly under his spell, regardless of whether or not they entirely approved of his more wayward interpretations. Some, of course, would never adjust to the impulsive spontaneity and dramatic force of a Mahler performance be it in the opera house or concert hall. The so-called 'truth' of the traditional Richter school of conducting had taken hold too deeply. Indeed, prior to Mahler's arrival, some conductors actually favoured a layout in the orchestra pit whereby the podium was placed with the orchestra *behind* it, presumably to effect a more immediate contact with the singers but, in the process, losing all eye contact with the orchestra. One can imagine how appalled Mahler would have been at the prospect of, quite literally, turning his back on the orchestra during a performance!

The immensity of Mahler's personal responsibilities in Vienna meant that precious composition time was once again dwindling. 1897 and 1898 were indeed fallow years. There was a limit to what one man – even a man of Mahler's remarkable stamina – could do: 'The sideline has become my main job', he told Justine and Natalie Bauer-Lechner, 'I no longer have the opportunity of time for the supreme task with which the Lord has entrusted me . . . I find it repugnant to live in the midst of all this splendour. How people admire me and grovel to me! How I'd love to tell them how miserably modest I feel and that in my job here, I want nothing but to do my duty'! The irony of the situation was, that for all his complaining, Mahler persisted in refusing to delegate any

The contrasting silhouettes of Richter and Mahler in action by Hans Schliessmann.

responsibility whatsoever. His totalitarian approach to just about everything he did was part and parcel of his own egocentricity. If something was to be done well, then one simply had to do it oneself.

One year after his arrival in Vienna, the area of his responsibilities extended still further to embrace the city's other major musical institution: the celebrated Philharmonic. Ostensibly for reasons of health, but perhaps too as an unconscious concession to youth – since it was perfectly clear that Mahler was far too single-minded an operator to share the position with anyone – Hans Richter stepped down as musical director, and set off en route for the Halle and London Symphony Orchestras in England. For Mahler this was not destined to be a happy liaison.

The Philharmonic, founded in 1842, maintained a dual complexion in Vienna. On the one hand, as resident orchestra in the pit at the Imperial Opera, it bowed to the whims of the musical director there, and on the other it wielded the iron fist of self-government – a system whereby each player, as a shareholder in the orchestra, was democratically entitled to voice an opinion on all matters of policy, financial or otherwise; to elect a board of governers from among its own members and, in turn, a musical director of its own choosing. The Philharmonic was, then, under absolutely no compulsion to elect Mahler. In fact, in the light of the controversy surrounding his first year at the opera this would seem to have been a curious move on their part. Stylistically he and Richter were poles apart. Richter had brought the orchestra to a pitch of perfection that few in the world could equal, let alone surpass, but he had done so by way of his own strictly orthodox methods, and whilst it might have appeared odd if the Philharmonic had chosen to overlook the internationally acclaimed celebrity on their doorstep, it must have been obvious from the start that Mahler was hardly likely to tread the same paths as his predecessor. Their very appearances on the rostrum said as much:

'In place of the tall-standing, blond-bearded giant who stood before the orchestra imperturbable, solidly built, broad and calm, a slender, nervous figure, possessing extraordinarily supple limbs, balanced itself on the podium'.

(From a review of critic Max Kalbeck).

Mahler's conducting technique mellowed greatly as the years went by, but up to, and including, the early part of his time in Vienna his rostrum manner, as we have seen, was one of quixotic impulse and nervous excitement:

'When the house grew dark, the small man with the sharply chiselled features, pale and ascetic looking, literally rushed to the conductors desk. His conducting was striking enough in his first years of activity in Vienna. He would let his baton shoot forward suddenly, like the tongue of a poisonous serpent. With his right hand, he seemed to pull the music out of the orchestra . . . He would let his stinging glance loose upon a musician who was seated far away from him, and the man would quail. Giving a cue, he would look in one direction, at the same time pointing the baton in another . . . He would leap from his conductor's chair as if he had been stung. Mahler was always in full movement, like a blazing flame'.

('Legend of a Musical City' – Max Graf).

Mahler's first appearance at the helm of the Vienna Philharmonic – in concert – took place on 6th November 1898. The programme, which featured Beethoven's Coriolan Overture, Mozart Symphony No. 40 and Beethoven Symphony No. 3, *The Eroica*, was designed with some cunning on Mahler's part. Richter had made his much lamented farewell to the Philharmonic with the Beethoven 3rd Symphony, so by including it in his first official programme Mahler was, in fact, presenting Vienna with something of a two-fold *fait accompli*: continuity would be preserved, but a new interpretative era had definitely arrived:

'There was icy silence at the entrance of the new conductor, and even after the towering Coriolan Overture, a breathtakingly dramatic performance, only sparse applause. Mahler's conception of the first movement of Mozart's G minor Symphony . . . found the audience more responsive. Then came the charming, floating Andante with its delicate ebb and flow; even the most hardened sceptics were conquered, and for the first time there was heartfelt applause . . . The climax of the concert, for sheer overall success, was the first movement of the *Eroica*. The immediate effect of Mahler's brilliant direction and of the magnificent playing of the Philharmonic was overwhelming, expressing itself in frantic bursts of applause'.

Thus reported critic Theodor Helm on the momentous first night, and one can see from his description just how readily Mahler's public were once again willing to put aside their prior conditioning and rise to the excitement of what was, after all, a dramatically new style of interpretation. The critics, of course, generally found it more difficult to lend an unbiased ear but, among their ranks too, the majority did at least acknowledge the freedom and theatrical force of Mahler's readings. As one of their most distinguished spokesmen, Eduard Hanslick, put it: 'All's well that starts well'; and this was certainly an auspicious start.

Sadly, Mahler and the Philharmonic never really developed a close working rapport. The players themselves offered little more than minimal respect to their new principal conductor and certainly the love that they extended to Richter simply never materialised. Ironically, Richter was every inch as much of a task-master as Mahler (his own daughter described him as a 'tyrant'), yet somehow his aura of respectability rose above the orchestra's retaliation. He was someone whose every word was to be unquestioningly revered, never challenged. He had a beard for a start which placed him among Vienna's senior citizens of wisdom, and more to the point, he was not Jewish. Every assertion that Mahler made, on the other hand, tended to be viewed as an act of arrogance and when he bore down on players, as he so often did, in the pursuit of something more from a performance – be it colour, characterisation or simply a

The Vienna Philharmonic Orchestra.

matter of instrumental balance – he would invariably run into a wall of resistance. At one rehearsal he repeatedly drove the orchestra over the opening of Beethoven's Fifth Symphony until a number of enraged players began packing their instruments to leave. 'Gentleman!', came the exasperated cry, 'save your fury for the performance. Then at least we will have the opening as it should be played!'.

Personality clashes aside, the Philharmonic never fully adapted to the radical stylistic changes that Mahler wanted to impose upon them. Had he initially handled what was an extremely delicate situation with kid gloves, then there might have been some chance of him winning their allegiance at an early stage in the relationship. As it was, he was prepared to make no musical compromises. That much had already been stated quite categorically. He continued to work on the assumption, or rather conviction, that he was always right, and the anti-semitic press, lobbied in opposition by the Jewish press, continued to fan the flames. It was a hopelessly unproductive climate in which to be working.

The area which not surprisingly brought about the biggest furore during this uneasy period was Mahler's re-touching of classical scores traditionally regarded as sacrosanct. The amendments that he made to the orchestrations in a number of the Beethoven symphonies, for instance, incensed the purist press and public alike to a storm of outrage. 'Barbarism', 'defamation' and 'treason' were among the random adjectives which were angrily, and somewhat irrationally, bandied about, yet none of these dissenters had even attempted to grasp the reasoning behind Mahler's actions, so blinkered were they by authenticity. The symphony orchestra had grown threefold since the days of Haydn and, with the advent of Berlioz, the string section alone necessitated an increase in the wind proportions in order to redress the balance. It was quite simply the question of clarity which preoccupied Mahler, himself a masterly orchestrator. Had sophisticated valve trumpets been available to Beethoven he might well have used them, as Mahler did, to double some of the choral writing in the Ninth Symphony. Similarly, given the larger string complement which had become common practice for performances of the symphonies, Beethoven would no doubt have strengthened his wind writing accordingly – again as Mahler did in the Fifth, Seventh and Ninth Symphonies.

In keeping a sense of proportion about this whole issue, one might remember that all Mahler's adjustments were purely concerned with reinforcing existing instrumental lines where changes in the size or character of the modern orchestra had created a textural imbalance. He had far too much respect of the work of others to have ever tampered with harmonic or melodic detail. Indeed, he had always maintained that should instrumental advances bring about a similar lack of clarity in his own scores he would readily thank anyone for making the necessary changes (though I wonder if he would actually have accepted this practice as readily as he preached it).

Similar, but more extensive, revisions took place later on the Schumann symphonies and as early as his fifth Philharmonic concert he led the entire string section of the orchestra in a performance of Beethoven's Quartet in F minor Op. 95. Far from avoiding a confrontation with his antagonists, Mahler appeared to be setting himself upon an inevitable collision course.

On February 18th 1900, he chose Beethoven's Ninth Symphony for the annual Nicolai concert in aid of the Philharmonic Benefit Fund. The ovation surpassed anything that he had thus far achieved in Vienna and the demand for tickets was so great that an immediate repeat performance was arranged. However, his own modifications to the score, in addition to those of Wagner, were intact of course and this factor, coupled with some of his notorious tempo flexibilities, drew a predicatble uproar from the critics. Even those who had been relatively courteous up until then finally lashed out at him. 'Instead of trying to understand Beethoven, Mahler should simply believe in him', came one response. Nobody, it seems, was able to appreciate that his departure from the customarily sedate style of Beethoven conducting grew out of conviction, not wilfulness. Prince Liechtenstein was among those present at the first performance and afterwards he was heard to say: 'A very beautiful performance, Herr Mahler, quite magnificent, and what a success! However, I have heard other tempos!'. 'Oh really, so your Highness has heard this work before?', was Mahler's cool retort.

The second performance was scheduled for February 22nd but Mahler had no intentions of allowing the vitriolic critical barrage of February 18th to go unanswered even if it meant widening the gap between he and his adversaries. In response to the accusations which had been levelled against him – in some cases through anonymous letters – the following leaflet was distributed at the entrance to the hall prior to the concert:

'As a consequence of certain published statements it is possible that certain members of the public might be led to conclude that the works of Beethoven, and in particular the Ninth Symphony, have been subjected to arbitrary alterations in matters of detail. It seems appropriate, therefore, to make an explanatory statement.

By the time his deafness became total, Beethoven had lost the intimate contact with reality, with the world of physical sound, which is indispensable to a composer. This happened at the very period in his creative life when the increasing power of his conceptions impelled him to

85

seek new means of expression and a previously unheard-of forcefulness in the treatment of the orchestra. This is well known, as is the fact that the construction of the brass instruments of the period rendered unplayable certain sequences of notes which were necessary to complete the melodic line. It was this same deficiency which ultimately occasioned the improvement of these instruments; and to fail to take advantage of this, in order to achieve perfection in the performance of Beethoven's works, would be perverse.

Richard Wagner, who endeavoured all his life, in word and deed, to rescue Beethoven's work in performance from an intolerable state of decadence and neglect, has shown in his essay 'On the performance of the Ninth Symphony of Beethoven' (Works, vol. 9) the way to achieve a performance of this symphony which is as close as possible to the intentions of its creator. All recent conductors have followed Wagner's lead; the director of today's concert has done the same, out of a firm conviction acquired and fortified through his own experience of the work, and without essentially going beyond the bounds set by Wagner.

*There can of course be no question of re-scoring, altering or 'amending' Beethoven's work.* The long customary augmentation of the strings has long ago brought in its train an increase in the number of wind instruments which are there purely to reinforce the sound, and *have not in any way been allotted a new orchestral role.* In this matter, as in every point concerning the interpretation of the work as a whole or in detail, it can be shown by reference to the score (the more detailed the better), that the conductor, far from imposing his own arbitrary intentions on the work – but also without allowing himself to be led astray by any 'tradition' – has been concerned to identify himself completely with Beethoven's wishes, down to the most apparently insignificant detail, and to avoid sacrificing in performance, or allowing to be submerged in a confusion of sound, the least particle of the master's intentions'.

Vienna, February 1900.                                          Gustav Mahler.


The public, meanwhile, packed the hall for his every appearance. No end of extra performances and special Sunday matinees could fulfil the demand. Within a framework of established classics he also acquainted Vienna with his beloved Bruckner's Fourth, Fifth and Sixth Symphonies (the first complete performance of the Sixth), albeit variously cut; and his own works, too, of course: the First, Second and Fourth Symphonies.

1901 began well. On February 17th 'the child of sorrow' from Mahler's 20th year – *Das Klagende Lied* – finally received its first performance, in Vienna, to predictable enthusiasm from the audience and derision from the critics. On February 24th, however, following the 100th Anniversary Performance of Mozart's *Die Zauberflöte*, Mahler collapsed and almost died from a sudden and very severe haemorrhage brought about by his recurring haemorrhoids. Not only his composition projects had been suffering during those busy winter months. He had woefully

'Mahler's metamorphoses': a newspaper caricature by Theo Zasche alluding to Mahler's alleged 'borrowings' from other composers. The caption reads: 'After the performance of his last symphony, several critics noted that Mahler could not free himself from the memories of the masters he esteems . . . At each new performance of his work, Mahler now presumes that he resembles, in facial expression and attitude, the composers who have influenced the particular composition'.
*From top left clockwise* Wagner, Liszt, Mahler orchestrating a folk-song as a bright spark from Vienna, A Viennese Beethoven, Schubert, Meyerbeer.

neglected his health, too, and in one sense the current crisis came as a sharp and timely reminder. In another, it indirectly provided him with a way out of his troubled relationship with the Philharmonic.

Whilst convalescing in Abbazia on the Adriatic, two of the remaining concerts of the season were allocated, in his absence, to Joseph Hellmesberger, son of the former director of the Conservatory, Franz Schalk, and Mahler's assistant. The critics were pointedly lavish in their praise. These, they proclaimed, were the finest performances to have been heard in Vienna since Richter's departure: worthy examples of good, solid 'classical tradition'. Hellmesberger's 'lack of individuality', emphasised one paper, was a small price to pay for a welcome return to sound craftsmanship. 'Good old musical blood, without wilfulness' were among other such phrases liberally peppered throughout the notices. Just how Mahler must have felt at seeing two very mediocre talents lauded to the skies at his expense, goes without saying.

On the advice of his doctors, however, he had already half-resolved not to stand for re-election to the conductorship of the Philharmonic. The rift between them had grown to be irreconcilable and he realised that without a unanimous vote of confidence from the players (which not even Richter had secured) the situation could only worsen. It was not difficult to make the break. Rationing his appearances with the orchestra might actually bring about, he thought, a greater appreciation of his ideals in the long run, and in any event, time of his own was becoming more precious by the minute.

In the summer of 1899 Mahler had taken to a well-known resort on the Alt-Aussee, noted for its tranquility and thermal baths. in an attempt to begin work on his Fourth Symphony. He had met with little success. The distractions were manifold. Travellers, many of whom knew and recognised him, came from far and wide to sample the salt-bath therapy and accordingly the village had insisted upon installing a municipal band for their entertainment. Add to disturbances of this nature that the weather was cold and Mahler's rented villa poorly heated and one quickly sees that what, in theory, had been intended as a tonic for his weary body, had rapidly turned out to be quite the reverse. Seclusion of his own choosing seemed once again to be the only possible solution. Instinctively he knew that the inspirational deadlock he was encountering over the fourth symphony had as much to do with his surroundings as anything else.

So, by August, serious house-hunting was the order of the day. Justine and Natalie Bauer-Lechner initially set about the task between themselves but were joined shortly afterwards by Anna von Mildenberg who had been brought up in the tiny province of

Maiernigg on the Worthersee and saw it as a distinct possibility. It was she who took them there and it was she, furthermore, who came up with the suggestion of a young amateur architect, one Alfred Theuer, who was willing and able to build a house quickly and at relatively low cost.

Mahler arrived shortly afterwards but it was some time – indeed, almost at the point of the idea being abandoned – before the ideal spot was found: a totally isolated and idyllic corner of the lakeside beneath a wild, primeval forest. 'It is too beautiful: one shouldn't allow oneself such a thing', Mahler apparently exclaimed looking down from the balcony of his quarters on the first day of his arrival there in 1900. The fourth symphony would pose no further problems for him now.

Just as the second and third symphonies took one of the *Wunderhorn* songs and used it as a kind of emotional climacteric to the surrounding whole, so the Fourth, too, germinated from a *Wunderhorn* setting: *Das Himmlische Leben* (The Heavenly Life) – the would-be seventh movement of his Third Symphony and now the final movement of his Fourth.

So fascinated was Mahler by the idea behind this poem – heaven viewed through the eyes of a child – that he decided to take the whole concept one stage further and conceive the entire work through the eyes of an innocent, as it were. Influenced no doubt by certain neo-classical trends which were sweeping the musical world at the time, he also scaled down his instrumental forces to a chamber-like transparency. There are no trombones or tuba in the Fourth Symphony and only triple wind; none of his other symphonies would be thus scored.

The Fourth is too often dubbed the happiest, the least troubled of Mahler's symphonies, possibly because it is shorter and more instantly tuneful and accessible than the others. The illusion, though, is a deceptive one. Far from being 'untroubled', its pastoral freshness and general air of contentment conceal no end of darker shadows. One simply sees them – as musicologist and Mahler specialist, the late Deryck Cooke so eloquently put it – from within this innocent, pastoral world 'as figures moving behind a veil which obscures their naked horror and makes them like the bogeymen who appear in illustrations to books of fairy tales'.

The Fourth was completed on 5th August 1900 leaving Mahler clear to begin work on his Fifth the following year. Of all his summer recesses, none was more productive than that of 1901. In addition to work on the new fifth symphony, he composed and orchestrated no less than seven lieder: *Der Tamboursg'sell* (The Drummer Boy) from the *Wunderhorn* series, three of his *Kindertotenlieder* (Songs on the Death of Children) and three more songs from poems by the romantic miniaturist, Friedrich Rückert.

88

One of these – *Ich bin der Welt abhanden gekommen* (I am lost to the world) – later came to be regarded as perhaps the most personal and poignant of all Mahler's lieder. To some extent he always looked upon it as autobiographical, yet never was he able to define this precise feeling in words: 'It's the feeling that fills one and rises to the tip of one's tongue but goes no further', he wrote later. The prevailing mood throughout most of these songs – among his greatest achievements in the field – was again mournful. Of the *Kindertotenlieder*, Mahler himself confessed: 'It hurt me to write them and I grieve for the world which will one day have to hear them, so sad is their content'.

The Fifth Symphony marked the start of what might be described as Mahler's 'middle period': a triptych of purely orchestral symphonies far removed from the fairy-tale fantasies, the explicit 'programmes', the folk inspirations, the voices and songs of their predecessors. We are confronted now with a new-found realism. The orchestrations take on a starker, more abrasive character, the structures, a greater sense of order and unity. One can feel a sudden determination on Mahler's part to confront reality, not hide behind the cosy complacency of past naiveties.

The Fifth is something of a split personality in musical terms. It opens with a weighty funeral march of harrowing intensity and closes in a spirit of unbridled joy. In between, and acting as a kind of transitional bridge from extreme darkness into extreme light, is the extraordinary central scherzo – a complex melting-pot, if you like, rich in quixotic transformations of mood and an air of mystical uncertainty.

This was one of the two movements that Mahler was able to complete in the summer of 1901 and there was to be nothing like it in the whole of his symphonic output. Of it, he wrote at the time: 'It's so thoroughly kneaded that there's not a single grain in it which isn't blended and transformed. Each note is endowed with supreme life and everything in it revolves as though in a whirlwind or the tail of a comet . . . I see it is in for a *peck* of troubles! Conductors for the next fifty years will take it too fast and make nonsense of it; and the public – oh, heavens, what are they to make of the chaos of which new worlds are for ever being engendered? . . . What are they to say to this primeval music, this foaming, roaring, raging sea of sound?'.

For the rest of 1901 Mahler's fortunes were equally well-starred. In September, his disciple and friend, 24-year old Bruno Walter, became his assistant at the opera and on November 25th, the Fourth Symphony received its eagerly awaited première in Munich. Mahler was now at the height of his popularity with the Viennese public and Walter recalls how even the city's taxi drivers would shout 'Long live Mahler!' whenever they spotted him. His enemies,

Mahler and Bruno Walter in conversation.

too, were at last having to sit up and take note.

Where Walter was concerned, Mahler was more than generous when it came to assigning repertoire. Doubtless he could remember all too clearly some of his own piecemeal assignations in the past, but that apart he had enormous confidence in the potential of his young protégé. Of course, the fact that Walter was young and Jewish was more or less guaranteed to draw the hostility of the press, and did. That he was a friend of Mahler's, too, was tantamount to treason. At the beginning, he was inevitably branded by some as an imitator of Mahler's style, and anti-semitic slights at Mahler were very often directed through him in this way. But Walter's work did grow in assurance and individuality under Mahler's watchful eye and the musical world can now remember him with affection as not only the undemonstrative, unaffected and thorough musician that he was, but also as a supreme interpreter of Mahler's music. The first performances of both the Ninth Symphony and *Das Lied von der Erde* (Song of the Earth) were entrusted to him after Mahler's death.

For Mahler, by far the most significant event of 1901 was a dinner party of the 7th November at the home of some newly acquainted friends of his: the Zuckerlands. There, amidst a

90

Alexander von Zemlinsky.

distinguished gathering, Mahler caught sight of a beautiful 22-year old girl – Alma Maria Schindler, daughter of the landscape painter Emil J. Schindler, who died in 1892, and stepdaughter of Carl Moll, one of the founders of the 'Secession' group with whom her mother had re-married five years after her father's death.

Their initial meeting was far from gracious. Indeed, during the course of the evening a heated argument errupted between them on the matter of a ballet score which Alexander von Zemlinsky (with whom Alma – also a musician – was studying) had submitted to Mahler for consideration. Mahler had apparently failed to so much as acknowledge the piece on the grounds that it was 'trash' musically and insupportable nonsense as a story, and it was on this issue that Alma angrily reproached him. There could be no excuse, she rightly pointed out, for his appalling rudeness in holding on to someone else's work for almost a year without comment, and that as far as the plot was concerned there were far greater absurdities currently on display in the Vienna ballet repertoire which she would be interested to hear him justify.

Mahler's immediate reaction to this spirited little tirade was, of course, one of instant admiration. He smiled broadly, Alma recalls, extended his hand in peace, and promised that he would call Zemlinsky in to see him first thing the following day. Alma related later how, as the guests gradually dispersed, she and Mahler remained alone as if separated from everyone else 'by that space created around themselves by two people who have found one another'. He enquired about her studies and requested that he be permitted to see some of her work one day soon. An invitation was then extended to her and her hosts to be his guests at a dress rehearsal of *The Tales of Hoffman* the following morning at the opera house and, with one final request that he be granted the pleasure of walking her home (which was declined on account of the late hour), he departed: bewitched.

# 8. Vienna II

'He had wielded power so long, encountering only abject submission on every hand, that his isolation had become loneliness'.

*Alma Mahler*

'You must understand that I could not bear the sight of an untidy woman with messy hair and neglected appearance. I must also admit that solitude is essential to me when I am composing; as a creative artist I require it without conditions. My wife would have to agree to my living apart from her, possibly several rooms away, and to my having a separate entrance. She would have to consent to sharing my company only at certain times, decided in advance, and then I would expect her to be perfectly groomed and well dressed. Finally, she should not take offence or interpret it as disinterest, coldness or disdain if, at times, I had no wish to see her. In a word, she would need qualities that even the best and most devoted women do not possess.'

Mahler was nothing if not honest in respect of his own chauvinistic frailties. Long before even contemplating marriage, he plainly evisaged a life of self-sacrifice for his future wife. Someone who would shoulder his domestic burdens, bear his children, copy his music, share his triumphs, his disappointments, his pain. Alma Schindler was destined for such a role.

Of her extraordinary and turbulent marriage to Mahler, she has, through her books, provided us with a wealth of illuminating detail and insight into the man who so irresistibly captivated her. Like all emotionally involved parties, though, one must sometimes approach her highly coloured, but somewhat humourless and often distorted oberservations with a degree of caution.

Certainly the world will always be indebted to her for the influence that she exerted over Mahler's music. To her credit she was able to recognise and eventually accept that he really only truly sublimated through music alone and that ultimately no-one, but no-one, could ever serve a higher purpose in his life than to act as an inspiration, a sounding board and a support for his creative tasks. It was a frustratingly passive role to play but one which, in Alma's case, commanded enormous authority. She spurred him to even

*Opposite* Alma Maria Schindler at the time of her meeting with Mahler in 1901.

93

greater heights than he had previously known. She became his motivation and his anchor at one and the same time. A month after they were married, he wrote from Berlin:

'I should like now to have success, recognition, and all those other really quite meaninless things people talk of. I want to do you honour.'

Alma's sexual proclivities have been endlessly, and perhaps sometimes unfairly, discussed and even satirised since her death in 1964. She was indeed a very seductive woman who lived life to the hilt and over the years lured a catalogue of the most distinguished suitors to her side. Before Mahler there was Gustav Klimt and her teacher, Alexander von Zemlinsky. Later, painter Oskar Kokoschka and architect Walter Gropius (founder of the Bauhaus) whom she finally married in 1915 after a harrowing affair which caused Mahler no end of pain during his last year; and, finally, her third and last marriage to writer Franz Werfel, with whom she eventually settled in the USA.

One common denominator links all these accomplished men. Each was touched with an intangible spark of genius and it was undoubtedly to this which Alma, above all else, was so compulsively drawn. Possibly she saw in such artists the way to enriching and extending the boundaries of her own intellect. Possibly they acted, too, as a form of substitute for those things that she felt she would never achieve herself. By all accounts she was a not untalented musician herself, for instance, yet in marrying Mahler she was perfectly prepared to sacrifice, at his demand, her own compositional pursuits in order to be at the service of his 'higher' ideals. Mahler was 'the purest, the greatest genius' that she had ever met. She passionately hoped that he would 'raise her to his level'.

Alma was already pregnant when she and Mahler married on the 9th March, 1902. The very next day, sister Justine was married to Arnold Rosé, leader of the Vienna Philharmonic – a liaison that had been taking place secretly for some time, much to Mahler's chagrin when he finally discovered the truth. His position with the orchestra was precarious enough without untoward family involvements further complicating the issue. In one respect Justine's marriage was probably just as well. Her near-pathological jealousy towards all women that came into Mahler's life would surely have become intolerable given Alma's similarly possessive nature. When considering the sacrifices that Alma makes such great play of in her writings, one should look, too, at the other side of the coin. She openly disapproved of many of Mahler's older acquaintances, particularly if they were female. It is certainly no coincidence that both Anna von Mildenburg and Natalie Bauer-

Mahler with Arnold Rosé, leader of The Vienna Philharmonic.

Lechner rapidly faded from prominence in Mahler's life after his marriage. No doubt Miss Bauer-Lechner's diaries would otherwise have provided us with some intriguing insight into his years with Alma, but seen from a quite different angle.

Their first year of marriage was everything they might have hoped. The honeymoon was spent in Russia and for the first time Alma was able to sit behind the orchestra during his three concerts in St. Petersberg and really watch Mahler, the conductor, in action.

'His exaltation when he was conducting was always intense and the sight of his face on these occasions, uplifted and open-mouthed, was so inexpressibly moving.'

In June she was at his side on the occasion of what was, in effect, his first unqualified triumph as a composer: the premiere of his Third Symphony in Krefeld. This was probably the single greatest turning point towards a genuine enthusiasm for Mahler's music outside Vienna. For Alma, it marked an indelible commitment to his art:

'I sat somewhere among strangers, for I wanted to be alone and had refused to sit with my relations. My excitement was indescribable; I cried and laughed to myself and suddenly felt the movement of my first child. I was so utterly convinced of Mahler's greatness by this work that night, amid tears of happiness, I swore to him my recognition of his genius, the love that wanted only to serve him, my eternal desire to live for him alone.'

Gustav Klimt

The summer of that first year established a pattern for the next five, and if Alma had not realised by now exactly what was to be entailed in her commitment to, or rather subservience to, Mahler's art, then she was about to find out. To her credit, she grew to understand the all-embracing creative force in Mahler that gave rise to his selfish egocentricity. There were times when she would resent it but, deep inside, she at least appreciated the cause:

'Work, exaltation, self-denial and the never-ending quest were his whole life on and on and for ever . . . He noticed nothing of all it cost me. He was utterly self-centred by nature, and yet he never thought of himself. His work was all in all.'

Bruno Walter once said that Mahler 'loved humanity but often forgot about man'. Alma was to know the true meaning of those words.

The routine in Maiernigg was much the same as it had been in Steinbach, the emphasis once again on work and only the bare essentials of living. Mahler's *hauschen* was again sparsely equipped: a large work table, a chair, a piano and a few bookshelves. He would

Villa Mahler at Maiernigg where Mahler spent the summers from 1900-1907 working on his Fourth, Fifth, Sixth, Seventh and Eighth Symphonies.

be installed there by 7 a.m. each day and work through until lunch when he would return to the land of the living and join Alma for a swim, a brisk walk, a row on the lake or simply an hour or so's sunbathing before eating. A notebook was always on hand lest some musical phrase or idea come to him while he was relaxing or exercising.

Contrary to some of the implications put forward by Alma herself, and but for his recurring throat and haemorrhoid problems (and those the result of inadequate medical facilities at the time), Mahler was actually very fit physically. How else would he have been able to sustain the immense pressures to which he was subject. There was really no time to regard illness with anything other than scorn. He trained like an athlete for his work, taking care not to abuse his body through careless diet or slovenly living. The rowing, the walking, the climbing, the swimming, were all geared towards greater physical fortitude and mental alertness.

By the end of the summer, the Fifth Symphony was completed in short score. Each day Alma would put her musical talents at the service of her husband and make fair copy of whatever he had completed that day. The anticipation of sharing in the creative process excited her enormously. During the remainder of the year Mahler would finalise his orchestrations, working before breakfast as part of an equally punctilious autumn and winter timetable in Vienna; rising at 7, he was in his office at the opera by 9; lunch was at 1 and tea at 5. There was no room for approximation on any of these times, so woe betide anyone who tampered with the schedules. Suffice it to say that the Mahlers' life-style in Vienna was a very far cry from the simple joys of their summer retreat. Home was now a luxurious flat in the Auenbruggergasse.

Mahler's European reputation grew with a vengeance during 1903. A triumphant candlelit performance of his 'Resurrection' Symphony in Basle Cathedral was undoubtedly one highlight of the year, but preceeding that was his first collaboration with the celebrated Concertgebouw Orchestra of Amsterdam and their principal conductor, Willem Mengelberg: a musician of striking temperament and already a devout Mahlerian. For Mahler and the orchestra it was love at first sight. Their performance of the Third Symphony in the October of that year had Amsterdam, indeed the whole of Holland, eating out of Mahler's hand:

'The tumult of applause was almost daunting. Everyone said nothing like it could be remembered. I have beaten Strauss, who is all the rage here, by yards!'

By 1904, Amsterdam was very much a 'Mahler city' – a tradition that not only Mengelberg but several of its distinguished

96

conductors since, not least Bernard Haitink, have carried through to the present day.

It is interesting, but to some extent puzzling, that Mengelberg should have become so favoured in Mahler's eyes as an interpreter of his music, if only on the evidence of his loving but wildly erratic recording of the Fourth Symphony, which still exists as a point of reference for us. Mengelberg, like Mahler, belonged very much to the school of free interpretation, and whilst he was no doubt closer to Mahler's conception of a true conductor than many of the 'metronomic' time-beaters, his flagrant disregard of Mahler's very specific tempo, phrasing and dynamic markings – in the case of this gramophone record – would surely have been greeted with some disapproval by the master. On one occasion, in Amsterdam, the Fourth Symphony was actually given twice in the same programme: first with Mahler conducting and then with Mengelberg – each a reflection of the other's interpretation. It could be that at this time Mengelberg's mannerisms were less excessive than they were when he came to make the recording. Or perhaps Mahler's immense admiration for his work allowed him some privileged degree of freedom from the letter of the score. We shall never know. We have only Mahler's unequivocal words to Alma: 'Mengelberg is a man you can rely on. I have friends here'.

Therein lies a sad irony, for it was Mengelberg who later stood by while Hitler's henchmen systematically sifted out all the Jews from the Concertgebouw Orchestra. It was he, too, who reputedly sent a personal telegram of congratulations when the Nazis took Paris. Fortunately these were betrayals that Mahler never lived to see.

In the summer of 1903, the Mahlers' second child was conceived, and on June 15th, 1904, Anna – nicknamed Guckerl – was born in Vienna. Spurred on in his elation, Mahler was enormously productive at Maiernigg that year. The Sixth Symphony, whose opening two movements he had sketched the previous year, was completed along with the two *Nachtmusik* movements from the new Seventh Symphony and two final settings to add to the existing three of his *Kindertotenlieder*.

The sentiments behind these lieder, bearing in mind that Friedrich Rückert had written the texts to bewail the loss of his own child, disturbed Alma to the point of anger. One can appreciate her feelings. To offer 'Songs on the Death of Children' when his own wife had barely recovered her strength after the birth of their second offspring would seem to have been excessively poor timing on Mahler's part. 'For heaven's sake, don't tempt providence!' she reproached him, and sure enough her words were to carry tragic significance within three years.

'Tragic' was in fact the subtitle by which Mahler's Sixth Symphony became known, though true to form he later dropped it.

Willem Mengelberg.

Sixth Symphony – the first
page of Mahler's autograph
score.

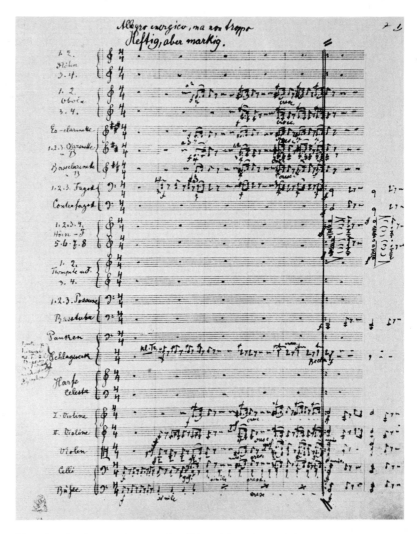

Despite its large time-scale (80 minutes) and hugely augmented
orchestra (eight horns, six trumpets, four trombones), this was
certainly the most classical of his symphonies: the first to adopt a
conventional four-movement form centred on one key – A minor.
Emotionally, he penned nothing more despairing, more utterly
pessimistic. With it he mourned all humanity. Little light
permeates its climatic finale – a voluminous and harrowing creation,
itself playing for some thirty minutes. The unseen hero of the
movement – inescapably an autobiographical as much as a universal
figure – strives bravely forward in perpetual but pointless
determination only to be struck down three times by cruel blows of
fate, 'the last of which fells him as a tree is felled'. It was for these
moments that Mahler took the unprecedented step of introducing a
'sledgehammer' effect into the score. Defiant march music twice
takes the movement to a pitch of 'all-or-nothing' exultation, but
twice, just as it looks as if victory might be in sight, the hammer

falls and with it the movement's 'fate' motive roaring out on the trombones, lacerating trumpets above it in two-part counterpoint. A third hammer-blow was originally placed to usher in the black, dissonant coda: a grim threnody of quietly intoning trombones finally obliterated by one shattering reminder of the Symphony's 'tragic' motto – a march rhythm from the timpani buttressed by trumpets in a major triad falling to a minor one.

Mahler's personal involvement in the catastrophic tragedy of this music was plain from the moment he set to work on it. He was beset with premonitions. The birth of his second child, the insecurities of his love for Alma, sexual fears and jealousies, all contributed to the potency of the utterance. The second subject of the first movement is Alma's music: a soaring theme for the violins, richly embellished by horns but prophetically swept away like a husk in the wind by the ugly tramping march music which opens the work. Only in the first movement does the menace momentarily subside. Suddenly we are transported from earthly strife to one of those mountainous regions so much a part of Mahler's peace of mind and refuge. Distant cowbells are heard: 'the last terrestial sounds penetrating into the remote solitude of mountain peaks', as Mahler once put it. But the peace is short-lived and overall there is little hope to be found anywhere.

'Not one of his works came as directly from his innermost heart as this. We both wept that day. The music and what it foretold touched us deeply . . . ' wrote Alma, recollecting how Mahler had played through the symphony for her that summer and how disturbingly fatalistic it had all seemed. Indeed, however cynically one might view questions of superstition and prediciton, it would certainly seem as though Mahler was mapping-out his own destiny with this music. A year after the première, three savage blows of fate *did* befall him: circumstances forced his resignation at the Vienna Opera, his dearly beloved daughter Maria died at the age of only four-and-a-half, and a few days later his doctor diagnosed the heart defect from which he would eventually die. Mahler was anyway acutely superstitious, so just as he later removed the numbering from what was, in effect, his Ninth Symphony – *Das Lied von der Erde* – in an attempt to evade the ominous stigma attached to ninth symphonies (Bruckner, Schubert and Beethoven had not lived to complete a tenth), he decided to delete the final hammer blow from his Sixth Symphony. No end of subterfuge, though, was going to cheat or even forestall the inevitable. The Ninth Symphony, proper, was still to be his last.

'I don't know anybody who can do more than I can', Mahler had bragged during that summer of 1903 – and justifiably so. Emotionally spent or not, he went straight from Maiernigg to Vienna in preparation for the launch of his magnificent *Fidelio*

Caricature on Mahler's Sixth Symphony poking fun at its battery of unusual percussion instruments. The caption reads: 'Good God! Fancy leaving out the motor horn! Ah well, now I have an excuse for writing another symphony'.

The Mahlers out walking near Toblach, 1909.

production in collaboration with Alfred Roller. The same season saw a belated production of Hugo Wolf's *Der Corregidor*, which Alma referred to as a 'debt of honour' in view of the remorse which Mahler still felt over the rift between him and Wolf: a rift which may or may not have contributed to Wolf's subsequent insanity. *Der Corregidor* was not a success. Mahler called it 'an opera of songs' and of Wolf's songs he was hardly complimentary: 'I know only 344', he was once reputed to have said, 'Those 344 I do not like'.

Shortly before the première of his Fifth Symphony, scheduled for 18th October, 1904, in Cologne, a play – through of the work was arranged with the Vienna Philharmonic. Alma, who by now knew the score intimately, having so laboriously copied every bar, sat in the hall and listened. She was horrified by ill-balances in the orchestration, in particular the overscoring of the percussion which she maintained – and Mahler agreed – swamped important thematic detail. Many revisions of the Fifth took place – more radical revisions than in any other Mahler compositions – but it was not until December 1905, in Vienna, that audiences began to grasp its mystifying extremes of mood and style. The absence of a programme meant that the listener was totally reliant upon his or her response to the piece as 'pure music', which, of course, made considerable demands upon their concentration and imagination.

Whilst he had predicted that the Fifth would pose problems, Cologne was still a major disappointment for Mahler. Bruno Walter, too, recalled it as the first and only time that a Mahler work

Adagietto.

Tacet

*Top* This cartoon inspired by the first Vienna performance of the Fifth Symphony shows the tuba player seizing his opportunity for a well-earned rest during the adagietto. *Bottom* Alban Berg and Arnold Schoenberg.

under the composer's baton had left him dissatisfied. 'The Fifth is an accursed work!' was Mahler's angry response after the Cologne premiere, 'No-one understands it'.

Understanding was not long in coming, though. Several performances followed in 1905, each increasingly successful, and as we have seen in recent years, one movement – the radiant adagietto for strings and harp alone – has become something of a cult among lovers of Mahler's music. For this we can partly either thank or reproach Luciano Visconti who put it to work on the sound track of his film of Thomas Mann's *Death in Venice*, controversially modelling the novel's central character, 'Aschenbach', on Mahler.

Vienna finally heard the Third Symphony in December 1904. Since Krefeld its trail had been blazing, so in a way it came as no surprise that the great capital should now think it timely to jump on the bandwagon and accord it similar recognition. Alma's young friend, Arnold Schoenberg (then aged 30), was just one among the many converted. A revolutionary voice himself, he saw and identified for the first time with this music's daring individuality and emotional potency:

'I saw your very soul naked, stark naked . . . I felt your symphony. I shared in the battling for illusion; I suffered the pangs of disillusionment; I saw the forces of good and evil wrestling with each other; I saw a man in torment struggling towards inward harmony . . . Forgive me, I cannot feel by halves.'

The unsuppressed excitement of those words convey something of the impact that this new and still strangely alien music was making at each successive performance. That they were written by one of Vienna's next generation of composers gives them added significance. Just as Schoenberg identified with the pioneering spirit in Mahler's music, so Mahler reciprocated. He did not always understand what it was that these youngsters of the new wave were trying to say, but he recognised a kindred spirit of adventure in their work and encouraged them accordingly. Mahler was of considerable moral and financial support to Schoenberg throughout his life, but I doubt that even he realised the extent of his influence in musical terms.

'The Second Viennese School', as it later became known, constituted a trio of composers: Schoenberg, Alban Berg – who in 1901, as a boy of 16, had rushed into Mahler's room after the first performance of the Fourth Symphony and carried off his baton as a momento – and Anton Webern. Their music was a natural progression from Mahler's own, not least in the way in which all three of them initially looked to similarly extravagant orchestral resources before moving on to a new-found economy of expression,

both in the size of the instrumental forces, the spareness of the
orchestration, and the systemisation of the melodic construction: a
process of atonality which became known as the twelve-note
method.

Had Mahler lived but a few more years, one wonders how far he
would have ventured along the same progressive path as these, his
immediate successors. Passages in the unfinished Tenth Symphony
(a substantial representation of which we are now able to hear in
Deryck Cooke's miraculous performing version) find him already
exploring similarly uncharted areas, though still firmly rooted, of
course, within the 'romantic' format wherein he thrived. It does
seem inconceivable that Mahler could ever have abandoned his
thoroughly 'romantic' leanings altogether. They constituted his
expressive centre without which he would doubtless have found
himself creatively impoverished.

The furthest that Mahler ever ventured along a truly
experimental path was unquestionably his Seventh Symphony: the
proverbial 'black sheep' among all his symphonic works and
certainly the least well known. Sandwiched between two shattering
masterpieces – the doom-laden Sixth and the heaven-storming
Eighth – is it any wonder that this curious hybrid has aroused so
much puzzlement and even suspicion over the years. Yet its place in
the Mahler canon is really quite logical when one considers how
quickly it followed the 'descent into Hell' of the Sixth Symphony
and how daunting it must have been for him to think in terms of
following that. Plainly the Seventh provided Mahler with a much-
needed reprieve from the emotional conflicts of his inner-self; an
opportunity to temporarily move away from spiritual motivations
into the realms of 'pure', 'absolute' music for its own sake. For once
there were no autobiographical connotations. His musical
imagination was free to run riot. He could look objectively at all the
trends that were taking place in modern music at the time and
formulate his own ideas around them. The results proved to be
enormously stimulating, if ultimately shallow. The Seventh is,
above all, a feast for the ear: as fantastic and kaleidoscopic a world
as Mahler ever conceived, its orchestrations dipping into a whole
new range of sonorities, revolutionary even by Mahler's standards.
For all its radical advancements, though – and harmonically, large
stretches of it foreshadow Mahler's very last works – there are
weaknesses here which suggest that, ultimately, Mahler was less
comfortable working 'outside' his normal genre, as it were. This
was the closest that he ever came to composing from the head rather
than the heart – and it shows.

Significantly, fears of inspirational sterility were never so great as
when he set about completing it in the summer of 1905. As he
wrote then to Alma:

Mahler in the Dolomites.

In art as in life, I am at the mercy of spontaneity. If I *had* to compose, not a note would come . . . I made up my mind to finish the Seventh, both andantes of which were then on my table. I plagued myself for two weeks until I sank into gloom . . . then I tore off to the Dolomites. There I was led the same dance, and at last gave it up and returned home . . . I got into the boat and rowed across. At the first stroke of the oars, the theme (or rather the rhythm and character) of the introduction to the first movement came into my head – and in four weeks, the first, third and fifth movements were done.

In the final analysis, and despite the brooding magnificence of its first movement, no-one is likely to dispute that the Seventh Symphony's pure gold lies at its heart in the two *Nachtmusik* movements and the equally nocturnal Scherzo. As for the finale, one wonders if even Schoenberg, who was wildly, and perhaps indiscriminately, enthusiatic about the whole piece, harboured any doubts about its outrageously rambling and chaotic nature, noisily dominated as it is by a mass of neo-baroque trumpet fanfares, incongruous dance tunes and vulgar switches of style.

I think Deryck Cooke has best conveyed, through his well chosen words on the central three movements, something of the strange world that this bizarre work inhabits:

. . . those superbly poetic stylisations of romantic genre pieces, which draw continually on the style of the period's popular music in the most subtly creative way. The prowling nocturnal patrol of the first 'Nachtmusik', amidst echoing horn-calls and the indeterminate noises of night; the Hoffmannesque spookiness of the scherzo, with its opposition between 'things that go bump in the night' and puppet-like waltz music; the gurgling streams, the tinkling guitar and mandoline serenades of the second 'Nachtmusik' – all these are haunting, uncanny music, opening magical windows on imagined worlds behind the visible world.

Of contemporary musical events during 1905, none was more sensational or controversial than the première of Richard Strauss' first mature opera *Salome* (Dresden, 9th December). Earlier in the year, Mahler and Alma had been treated to an impromptu sneak preview when Strauss whisked them into a local piano shop and proceeded to play and sing the entire piece: all, that is, but the 'Dance of the Seven Veils' which had still be be composed. Even then Mahler was in no doubt as to the work's calibre, an opinion that was further substantiated when he and Alma later travelled to Graz for the Austrian première. 'Undoubtedly one of the most magnificent works that has been produced in our time', was his verdict then and plans were immediately laid for an early Vienna staging; or rather, that was his intention until the censor intervened. Irrespective of the work's artistic merits, it seemed that Oscar Wilde's spicy re-telling of the notorious biblical text was considered unsuitable for respectable Viennese stomachs.

Mahler was furious. The whole episode was typical of Vienna's underhand hypocrisy. Emperor Franz Joseph was forever professing liberalism but beneath the surface the old repressive conservatism was grinding away. What perplexed Mahler most of all was the fact that his artistic integrity had been called to question over a work which he plainly held in such high esteem. The censor even suggested that 'in the interest of all concerned' he excercise discretion towards the press. It was yet another step closer to a complete erosion of his authority at the opera. The novelty of his presence there was plainly wearing thin. Intrigue and speculation were rife at his expense.

Meanwhile, the first performance of the Sixth Symphony was set for the 27th May 1906 at the Essen Festival. None of Mahler's symphonies were ever premièred in Vienna while he was alive. Sensibly, he was far too conscious of leaving himself open to further accusations of self-interest. The hawks, after all, were only too ready to swoop. Just as had been the case with the Fifth Symphony, a prior play-through of the Sixth was organised in Vienna. Once again someone – in this case a young Russian répetiteur in Vienna: Ossip Gabrilovitch – was assigned to take notes on Mahler's behalf so that any problems relating to internal clarity and textural balance could, to some extent, be cleaned up before rehearsals began.

A major priority in the case of the Sixth centred around finding the right non-metallic sound for those hammer blows in the finale. An enormous sound-box covered with stretched hide was constructed specially, but after various experiments involving clubs and mallets it was decided that an ordinary bass drum actually produced a more fearsome crack. Nowadays one sees percussionists and conductors going to extraordinary lengths to secure the right effect; any and everything, in fact, from road-pummellers to piano stools have been seen to appear on the platform!

A week of rehearsals preceeded the Essen première and at the last of these Alma was joined by Grabilovitch, one or two other friends, and Richard Strauss. According to Alma it was a deeply harrowing and overwhelming experience. 'You are in for a treat', Mahler had told her before the rehearsal, but not even he had fully anticipated the effect that this despairing cry from the depths of his own soul might have upon him – in retrospect, as it were. Alma recalls how after the rehearsal he 'walked up and down in the artists room, sobbing, wringing his hands, unable to control himself', while she and others froze at the spectacle, not daring to look at one another.

Apparently, it was into this delicate atmosphere that Richard Strauss then noisily burst bearing some trivial news about a small amendment to the following night's programme: 'I say, Mahler, you've got to conduct some dead march or other tomorrow before the Sixth – their Mayor has died on them. So vulgar, that sort of thing. But what's the matter? What's up with you?' Naturally, it would never have occurred to Strauss that Mahler's condition might just have been brought about as a direct result of the music's personal connotations. Just as he viewed his own work with a sense of detachment, so it is unlikely that he would have seen the Sixth on anything other than the level of its effects and showmanship. He even made a remark in passing to the effect that he thought the work was overscored in places – a criticism which, according to Bruno Walter, distressed Mahler greatly. In this work, above all, he had deliberately taken great pains to effect maximum transparency from his outsize wind compliment. 'Can't you play that any louder?' he had repeatedly shouted at his six trumpets during the course of rehearsals, when in fact the din in the empty hall was already quite ear-splitting. Yet, as always, there was method in his madness. Only when they were finally playing fit to burst at the points specified did order emerge out of apparent chaos, because only then were they truly dominating the tutti as his inner-ear had dictated.

Mahler was meticulous about leaving nothing to chance in the marking of his scores. Dynamic and expressive markings were explicit to a degree. An extremely low bass passage, essential to the colour of his scoring, might carry the note: 'Under no circumstances may this passage be played an octave higher than written'; or he might specify that a soloist enter 'almost inaudibly' (*'Beinahe unhörbar eintreten')*. Certainly he would always instruct his wind players at exactly which points they were to lift the bells of their instruments (*'Schalltrichter in die höhe')* so as to pull focus – both aurally and visually – on an important note or phrase. Music had come a long way since the baroque era when composers did not even always indicate which instrument was to play which part.

The summer recess of 1906 was to be a time for total relaxation and recuperation. At least that was what Mahler had firmly resolved. Still troubled by nagging fears that his creative powers may be dwindling, he was nonetheless determined that such fears should not grow to be obssessions. He would simply idle away the hours and conserve his energies until the time was ripe. An excellent philisophy, as it happened, but one that bore fruit sooner than he might have imagined. On the very first day of his holiday he took the traditional early morning stroll down to his hut:

'On the threshold of my old workshop the 'Spiritus Creator' took hold of me and shook me and drove me on for the next eight weeks until my greatest work was done.'

Eight weeks, then, was all it took to conceive and realise the monumental Eighth Symphony. A more eloquent manifestation of the mystical spiritual forces that appeared to guide and impel Mahler's creative hand at every turn of his career would indeed be hard to envisage. The so-called *Symphony of a Thousand* – so called on account of its vast choral and instrumental forces (a popular title, though, and not of Mahler's making) – was the first completely choral symphony ever to have been written, predating Vaughan Williams' 'Sea Symphony' by almost three years. In essence it could be said to represent a summation of Mahler's own humanitarian aspirations: his belief in the power of spiritual enlightenment to elevate mankind from the depths of failure, wrongs and despair through the highest Christian ideals of brotherhood, wisdom and love.

Mahler chose to structure his work in two complimentary parts,

106

the first comprising a tautly symphonic setting of the ancient hymn, 'Veni Creator Spiritus', the second an operatically-styled realisation of the final scene from Goethe's *Faust*. One can feel the impulse and force of Mahler's sudden inspiration in the mighty invocation of the very first bars: a fortissimo Eb chord for organ, woodwind and lower strings followed by a flood of choral sound with the opening words of the hymn — effectively the work's key motif. The irresistible momentum of this first movement is remarkable: its gigantic arc-like form as but a single prolonged phrase surging inexorably to its ecstatic apotheosis.

Part 2, though arguably a synthesis of adagio, scherzo and finale, enters a more romantic, rhapsodic world. An abundance of sensual texturing, mystical light and shade takes us closer to familiar Mahlerian territory. The scoring here is a model of clarity and subtle shading, not at all what one might expect at first glimpse of the vast choral and orchestral forces employed: a huge orchestra (quadruple wind, eight horns and 'extras' such as mandolin and harmonium), an extra brass complement placed separately from the orchestra, eight soloists, double choir (size as much as possible), boys' choir and organ. In fact, Mahler rarely calls upon their collective might for its own sake. Rather he explores a whole range of instrumental and choral combinations in order to secure chamber-like transparency in the orchestral writing and as near ideal a balance as possible between soloists, chorus and orchestra.

It is easy to see why he was so drawn to Goethe's text for the second part of his symphony. Other writers dramatising the 'Faust' story had sought only eternal damnation for its central figure. The humanistic Goethe, on the other hand, chose to look upon him as a symbol of questing humanity, a seeker of truth; one who strives for enlightenment and maybe fails through misguidance and folly, but one who — in spite of all — still succeeds in finding ultimate redemption.

The last eight lines of Goethe's text are transformed by Mahler into a timeless metaphysical vision of his own: a blazing religious chorale (Chorus Mysticus) which harkens back uncannily to the message of hope and salvation that he gave out so resplendently at the close of his Second Symphony (Resurrection). In the final coda, extra brass from 'on high' magisterially return to the symphony's opening theme in blinding transformation — its interval of the seventh now changed to a major ninth as if reaching out for the beyond. The grand eternal plan has come full circle.

It is the biggest thing I have done so far . . . Imagine that the universe begins to vibrate and to sound. These are no longer human voices but planets and sun rotating.

Mahler in a letter to Willem Mengelberg, 18th August, 1906.

For Mahler, the Eighth Symphony was but one shaft of light in a rapidly darkening world. 1907 closed in on him from all sides. In Vienna, storm clouds were gathering at the opera and the opposition, ever ready to strike, were demanding answers to some very pressing questions. Expenditure had risen and box office receipts were falling. Why then, it was asked, was the musical director spending so much of his time pursuing personal engagements elsewhere? And why was his collaborator, Alfred Roller, not being forced to curtail his extravagant expenditure on design when clearly the house could not hope to recoup his excesses? It was a sorry state of affairs given that standards had risen so immeasurably. Even Prince Montenuovo, who had hitherto upheld Mahler's interests against all comers, moved in to oppose him over the Roller issue.

Out of loyalty, Mahler defended Roller wholeheartedly – their artistic accomplishments together were, after all, beyond reproach – yet he knew, in truth, that his antagonists did have some grounds for complaint on both counts. For his own part, the demand for performances of his music all over Europe was now increasing at an unprecedented rate, and since experience had taught him never to entrust performances of his own works to others where it were possible to establish a tradition of interpretation himself, he was indeed spending more and more time away from Vienna.

Once again, it was a question of priorities, and Mahler, in all honesty, had never made any secret of where his lay. Now seemed to be the time for him to bow out graciously. Recent events were a sure sign that Vienna was growing bored with the novelty of their controversial Music Director and he, in turn, was tired of justifying his every move, his every decision:

All things have their day and I have had mine and so has my work as the local opera director. I am no longer 'news' so far as Vienna is concerned. So I want to go at a point when I can still expect that, at a later date, the Viennese will learn to appreciate what I did for their theatre.

Mahler finally tendered his resignation on 31st March 1907. The search for a replacement was not immediately fruitful. Indeed, a period of some unease and embarrassment followed during which Montenuovo actually asked Mahler if he would not reconsider his decision. On August 10th, however, it was announced that Felix Weingartner – the young conductor from Berlin that Mahler had stopped off to see during his international concert tour of 1897 – would step into the coveted position from the following January.

Details could now be made public of an offer which Mahler had

Felix Weingartner.

Mahler with his first
daughter, Maria Anna
('Putzi').

been harbouring for some time – an offer from no less than
Heinrich Conried, Director of the Metropolitan Opera, New York.
Initially, Conried had discreetly approached him with the
suggestion of a four-year contract, but at Mahler's insistence that he
could not commit himself to a new house, sight-unseen as it were,
for so long a period, a trial engagement of four months, at the
phenomenal salary of $20,000, was finally agreed upon (some
indication indeed of Mahler's earning power at the crest of his
success). Financially, Vienna too had been more than generous to
their outgoing Music Director: an inflated pension, a sizeable
compensatory payment of K 20,000, and special dispensation that
Alma be entitled to the pension of the widow of a Privy Councillor
in the event of Mahler's death.

Overshadowing all these complex negotiations, though, was the
nagging question of Mahler's health. In January of that year he

apparently consulted his family doctor Blumenthal, who discovered a slight valvular defect of the heart (a lesion). His advice, to avoid over-fatigue but attempt to carry on living as normally as possible, was reassuring but inconclusive. It is doubtful that doctors at the time would have made any connection between Mahler's recurrent throat infections and the appearance of a defect such as this, yet the two were in fact directly related. Subacute bacterial endocarditus – as the condition later became known – was, in essence, the legacy from Mahler's accumulative throat infections. Penicillin, which alas came seventeen years too late to be of any assistance to him, would have arrested the problem before it got out of hand.

Determined, nonetheless, to heed his doctor's advice, and satisfied also that the New York deal was now signed and sealed, Mahler took Alma and the children off to Maiernigg towards the end of June. Just three days after arriving, the cruelest blow of all struck. Their elder daughter, Maria ('Putzi') contracted a combination of scarlet fever and diptheria and suffered agonisingly for almost two weeks before finally succumbing, aged only four and a half. To lose her was terrible, but to see her suffer like this was simply unbearable. 'Putzi' symbolised for Mahler the childhood he had never known. Alma relates how they would play and talk endlessly together, 'nobody has ever known what about'.

Not surprisingly, Alma cracked physically under the shock and strain of those fearful two weeks, but it was only when Dr. Blumenthal was summoned to give her a thorough examination that the full extent of the toll taken on Mahler himself also became apparent. On re-examining him (which seemed sensible while he was attending to Alma), Blumenthal noticed a distinct worsening of the heart lesion that he had discovered only a few months earlier and suggested that Mahler consult a specialist, Professor Kovacs, in Vienna. Kovacs spelt out the seriousness of the condition in no uncertain manner. He had to conserve his strength if he was to stay alive.

To Mahler, of course, any restriction on his outdoor activities – his climbing, his swimming, his cycling – amounted to nothing short of a death sentence in itself. He may have underplayed the implications at first (and we have reason to believe that, for Alma's sake, he did), but for one who revelled so in the exhilaration of the open-air, this particular revelation was to hang like a black cloud over his remaining years. Death was no longer just an idea – a sinister, philosophical mystery on which he could fantasise – but a stark reality. The question now loomed large as to how he was likely to respond creatively, if at all, to this savage blow. In the event, his last great triptych of works – *Das Lied von der Erde*, the Ninth Symphony and the uncompleted Tenth – confirmed beyond doubt that his creative instincts had, if anything, been sharpened by his new-found awareness of impending mortality. Just where one might have predicted stagnation, decline, dissollusionment, instead – beneath their shadowy conflicts – breathed a sense of preparation, of resignation to his final destiny.

In an attempt to escape the catastrophic events of the preceeding weeks, Mahler and Alma sought refuge at Schluderbach in the Austrian Tyrol. There they spent the remainder of the summer. By way of a distraction, Mahler read *Die Chinesische Flöte* (The Chinese Flute), an anthology by Hans Bethge based on ancient Chinese poems. A friend had suggested earlier in the year that they might make interesting song settings; perceptively so, as it turned out, since it was from this collection that Mahler selected his texts for *Das Lied von der Erde*. According to Alma, he began making preliminary sketches during these very difficult weeks.

The autumn season at the opera was, of course, his last. On 15th October, to a disconcertingly thin house, he bade farewell with a performance of *Fidelio*, departing almost immediately afterwards for a concert trip to Russia. Between two dates in St. Petersberg he travelled to Helsinki, making yet more revisions to his Fifth Symphony en route in preparation for the second of the concerts on 9th November (a triumph apparently; Igor Stravinsky, who was in the audience, recalls the evening with enthusiasm. The programme also included some Wagner fragments and a work by Tchaikovsky – possibly the *Manfred* Symphony).

Helsinki was the scene of Mahler's now celebrated meeting with his distinguished contemporary, Jean Sibelius. For all their artistic differences, both men appeared to enjoy each other's company a great deal:

'As a man Mahler was extremely modest and an extraordinarily interesting person. I admired . . . his aesthetic greatness as a man and artist', commented Sibelius.

'An extremely pleasant person, like all the Finns', was Mahler's rather more sweeping generalisation.

The conversation, according to Sibelius, touched upon 'the great musical questions of life and death' and, perhaps more fascinatingly, a difference in attitude towards the nature of Symphony. It was in response to Sibelius' vigorous advocation of 'strictness and style' and a sense of profound logic in symphonic composition that Mahler made his now well-worn retort: 'No, the symphony must be like the world. It must embrace everything?'

In some respects, it is surprising that Mahler's admiration and goodwill towards his Finnish contemporary did not extend to the music. Surprising because here was another voice of distinctive individuality in respect of orchestral timbre and harmonic invention: another visionary artist with a flair for evoking sounds

Jean Sibelius.

which seemed to emanate directly from the very fibre of his magnificent homeland.

'Hackneyed clichés' was how Mahler summed up the Sibelius he heard in Helsinki (though there is some uncertainty as to what it was), but then he was often impulsive, even schizophrenic, when it came to passing judgment on the work of others. In one oddly ill-considered moment he was once quoted as rating Wagner's *Rienzi* among the composer's greatest work; Brahms, whom at one time he had placed above his revered Bruckner, was later referred to as being (in the musical sense, of course) 'a puny little dwarf with a rather narrow chest . . . It is seldom he can make anything of his themes, beautiful as they so often are'; and among the Italians, Puccini ('nowadays any bungler can orchestrate to perfection') was often held in very low esteem against many an inferior talent.

Mahler's official farewell to his loyal Viennese public took place on Sunday 24th November, 1907. An audience drawn from all walks of Vienna's musical life packed the great Musikvereinsaal for a performance of his Second Symphony. Not even Mahler could have envisaged so tempestuous a demonstration of approval as he received that night. Thirty times he was recalled to the platform. It was an occasion to move all but the hardest heart.

The next day – his last in residence at the opera house – this letter appeared on the notice board there:

Honoured Members of the Court Opera:

The time of our working together has come to an end. I leave a working community that has become dear to me and bid you all farewell. Instead of a complete, rounded whole, such as I had hoped for, I leave behind the incomplete, the fragmentary, as a man seems fated to do. It is not for me to judge what my work has meant to those for whom it was intended. But at this moment I can honestly say, I have tried my best, I have set my aims high. My endeavours were not always crowned with success. No one is so exposed to the perverse obstinacy of matter, to the malice of the object, as the interpretative artist. But I have always pledged all I have, putting the aim above my person, my duty before my inclinations. I did not spare myself, and therefore felt I could ask others to exert their full powers.

In the thick of the fray, in the heat of the moment, neither you nor I could escape altogether injuries or misunderstandings. But when our work was successful, a problem solved, we forgot all our troubles and felt richly rewarded, even if the outward signs of success were lacking. We have all of us made progress, and with us the institution we sought to serve. Accept my heartfelt thanks, then, to all who have supported me in my difficult, often thankless task, who have aided me and fought by my side. Accept my sincere good wishes for your future careers and for the prosperity of the Court Opera Theatre, whose fortunes I shall continue to follow with lively interest.

112

Sadly, though, neither these words nor the affirmation of the previous night did any thing to soften the dissenters. Mahler's farewell message was later found ripped from the wall and torn into pieces.

About two hundred well-wishers – among them Walter, Roller, Schoenberg and Zemlinsky – gathered at the railway station the following day: Monday 9th December. It was 8.30 in the morning when Mahler's train pulled away.

# 9. New York

*'Europe needs men like you as it does its daily bread'.*
*Gerhart Haumptmann.'*

Mahler's arrival in New York just one week before Christmas was preceeded by a flurry of publicity that surpassed even the New Yorkers' sensation-seeking best. Extreme crises demanded extreme measures and the Metropolitan had certainly fallen upon hard times. Its Director – the German-born and Vienna-trained Heinrich Conreid – was in poor health and the house was faced with an ever-growing challenge from Oscar Hammerstein's four-year-old Manhattan Opera House. Already this young and enormously successful company had succeeded in topping the Met's glittering array of stars by attracting to their own ranks the likes of Nellie Melba and Louisa Tetrazini.

Conreid may not have been the most musical of impressarios but he was certainly shrewd enough to realise that only someone of Gustav Mahler's standing in the operatic world could hope to salvage the Met from its current plight. A renewed burst of prestige was urgently needed and it was hoped Mahler would provide just that. Embarrassingly enough, Otto H. Kahn, one of the Met's major backers, had ideas of his own along similar lines, and at the very same time that Conreid was clinching the initial deal with Mahler in Berlin, Kahn was secretly in Paris lining up the infamous Giulio Gatti-Casazza, Director of La Scala, Milan, to succeed Conreid – the assumption being that Conreid's ill-health would soon force him to resign. The ulterior motive behind this move – the prize, as it were – was Arturo Toscanini, the fiery young Italian whose reputation was now spreading world-wide. With Gatti-Casazza assured for the Met, there was little doubt that Toscanini could be persuaded to follow him. At least that was the sensational coup that Kahn envisaged.

Needless to say, the Met's Board were now panicking, just a little, in anticipation of a Mahler/Toscanini confrontation. Not for nothing did Mahler's autocratic reputation precede his arrival wherever he went. Assurances from Gatti-Casazza that Toscanini

Mahler, 1911.

115

Arturo Toscanini.

Metropolitan Opera House, New York.

would accept the Mahler situation did seem a trifle optimistic, not to say premature. Toscanini had declared, it is true, that he would be happy to find himself 'with an artist of Mahler's worth. I hold Mahler in great esteem and infinitely prefer such a colleague to any mediocrity', but it remained to be seen whether the temperamental Italian would, in fact, practise what he was preaching.

In the event, it was not until the summer of 1908 that Gatti-Casazza finally took over from Conreid and, as we shall see, with the exception of one brief fracas over who should conduct *Tristan und Isolde* at the beginning of that season, Toscanini remained – for one season at least – a model of diplomacy in respect of Mahler's position.

'Where all others end, he begins . . . He has many peculiarities which cannot in any way be explained. As example, innumerable times I have seen men in his orchestra lay down their instruments absolutely like paralysed, unable to sound a note, the only cause being the look in his eyes. I have heard them say "I cannot play a note until you take your eyes off me". He can secure almost any effect he desires through those wonderful eyes. Not by reason of his personality, because I do not think that anyone would call it agreeable.'

116

*Left* Enrico Caruso.
*Right* Feodor Chaliapin.

Coloured no doubt by fashionable hearsay, the young American conductor, Walter Rothwell, based those observations upon what he had seen and heard of Mahler in Europe. In contrast, the Mahler that arrived in New York was a figure very much subdued by family tragedy and poor health. He no longer had the strength to attend to every minute production detail as he had done in Vienna. He demanded no less of his performers, it goes without saying, but for once he could detach himself to some extent from extraneous administrative headaches and adopt an easier going attitude to his duties. In effect, he could regard New York as a series of extremely lucrative guest appearances.

Enormously exciting, of course, was the calibre of artist at his disposal. Olive Fremstad (who sang her first 'Isolde' in Mahler's opening production; Heinrich Knote was the 'Tristan'), Johanna Gadski ('Brunnhilde' in his *Walküre* and *Siegfried*), Berta Borena ('Leonora' in *Fidelio*), Carl Burrian (the 'Florestan' in *Fidelio*), Antonio Scotti ('Don Giovanni'), Anton van Rooy ('Wotan' in the two *Ring* productions), Feodor Chaliapin and Enrico Caruso all featured during his first season, and patient New Yorkers who had been eagerly awaiting Mahler's much-trumpeted arrival were not, it seems, disappointed by the potency of those early performances.

117

*Tristan und Isolde* opened on 1st January, 1908. 'The influence of the new conductor was felt and heard in the whole spirit of the performance', wrote Richard Aldrich in the New York Times; 'Through it all went the pulse of dramatic beauty . . . a reading of the score that is comparable with the best that New York has known'.

Three weeks later, on 23rd January, came *Don Giovanni*, followed by *Die Walküre* on 7th February, *Siegfried* on 19th February and *Fidelio* on 20th March. For *Fidelio* Mahler used replicas of Alfred Roller's Vienna designs. He had hoped to transport the original sets over from Vienna in their entirety but the costs involved forced him to abandon that idea.

Mahler returned to Europe for a series of concerts and social calls in the summer of 1908. On the itinerary were stops in Vienna, Munich, Berlin, Hamburg, Paris, and Wiesbaden where he was to conduct his First Symphony. After the numbing events of 1907, it was naturally inconceivable that he and Alma should return to Maiernigg with its painful associations. But Mahler needed to work. He had composed nothing for over a year now and that in itself was hardly conducive to his mental well-being at a very difficult time. Alma, however, did manage to find a farmhouse in the Dolomites, just outside the village to Toblach, and they arrived there in June. She paints a very bleak and sad picture of that summer:

Mahler's house at Toblach.

118

'We were afraid of everything. He was always stopping on a walk to feel his pulse and he often asked me to listen to his heart and see whether the beat was clear or rapid or calm. I had often implored him to give up his long bicycle rides, his climbing and swimming under water, to which he was so passionately attached. There was nothing of that now. On the contrary, he had a pedometer in his pocket. His steps and pulse-beats were numbered and his life a torment. Every excursion, every attempt at distraction was a failure.'

For once, it seems, Alma was not over-dramatising the situation. A letter received by Bruno Walter at exactly this time finds Mahler in the depths of despondency:

'I must alter my whole way of life. You cannot imagine how painful this is to me. For years I have grown used to taking strenuous exercise, to walking in forests and over mountains and boldly wresting my ideas from nature. I would sit at my desk only as a peasant brings in his harvest, to give shape to my sketches. Even my spiritual worries disappeared after a long walk or a climb. Now I must avoid all effort, watch myself constantly, walk as little as possible. Living, as I do here, in solitude and concentrating on myself, I feel more intensely all that's wrong with me physically. Perhaps I'm looking on the black side, but since I've been in the countryside I've felt less well than in town, where distractions kept my mind occupied . . . As far as my 'work' is concerned, it is most depressing to have to unlearn everything. I have never been able to work only at my desk – I need outside exercise for my inner exercises . . . After a gentle little walk my pulse beats so fast and I feel so oppressed that I don't even achieve the desired effect of forgetting my body . . . This is the greatest calamity I have ever known.'

But solace did come as he became immersed once again in the Bethge songs that he had begun work on the previous summer. Their sorrowful mystique, their timeless philosophies somehow complimented his frame of mind. As he grew more and more engrossed in work on them, so his physical obsessions began to regress. Visitors to Toblach found him refreshed and mentally rejuvenated. His letters took on a more optimistic tone.

By 1st September the sixth song was completed in short-score and what had started out as a straightforward song-cycle had now grown, by way of more extended orchestral developments, into what was, in effect, a song-symphony – the forerunner of works like Benjamin Britten's *Spring Symphony* and Dmitri Shostakovich's Fourteenth Symphony which sprang later from precisely the same concept. He first intended to call his piece *Die Flöte Jade* (The Jade Flute). Later came *Das Lied von Jammer der Erde* (The Song of Earth's Sorrow) and then finally *Das Lied von der Erde* (The Song of the Earth).

Mahler came to look upon this as possibly the most personal of all his achievements. New horizons were opening up before him. At the twilight of his life, a process of 'learning' had begun again. 'Acclimatised' (as he put it to Walter) to the close reality of death, he had now found renewed delight in the beauty of nature and the sheer ecstasy of being alive. Every moment, every emotion now appeared heightened to him, as though crystalised for all eternity. Nowhere in any of Mahler's music are the bitterness of dying and the sweet sensuality of living juxtaposed in such perfect harmony.

The unique sound world of *Das Lied von der Erde* captures to perfection the distilled nature of Bethge's texts with all the fragile transparency of an oriental water-colour. Lines are finer, sharper – delicate and stark by turns – the quasi-Chinese atmospheres of the poems evoked with real harmonic ingenuity.

It is indeed miraculous that Mahler and 'The Chinese Flute' should have found each other at a time when they could express together so much of what he must have been experiencing. Nothing could encapsulate so poignantly the reluctant but dignified transition from life into death as 'Der Abschied' (The Farewell): the crowning adagio-finale of the work, itself equal in length to all the other movements put together.

This incomparable setting might best be described as Mahler's meditation on the finality of parting. Darkness, loneliness, longing, melancholy, resignation, are all somehow mingled and reconciled within its timeless pages. A sombre funeral march dominates (chilling colours from the depths of the orchestra : basses, contra-bassoon, horns and tam-tam); strange obligato woodwind solos ramble in solitary eloquence over sustained ground basses; elegaic and tragic is the mood, until finally, in a heart-felt and compassionate coda to words added by Mahler himself, it is as though he can no longer contain his longing for the life he loves so, but must leave: 'The dear earth everywhere blossoms in spring and grows green again. Everywhere and eternally the distance shines bright and blue. Eternally . . . eternally. . .' The soloist's final words – '*ewig. . . ewig*' – repeated over and over again fade to a barely discernable hush. Harp, celeste and mandolin alone weave a delicate thread around suspended pianissimo chords in the strings.

So remote, so far removed from this world are the closing bars, that it is almost impossible to determine the exact moment at which the music finally drifts into silence. Longing and resignation are finally at one.

The summer ended in higher spirits than it had begun with a visit to Prague for the first performance of the Seventh Symphony on 19th September. Alban Berg, Otto Klemperer, Walter Gabrilovitch and Artur Bodanzky were among many young musicians who had travelled there to sit in on the rehearsals. Their presence made for a joyful reunion which lifted Mahler's spirits no end. It had been three years since he completed this, the most bizarre of all his scores, and now more than ever he was torn with doubts over certain aspects of the piece. Various revisions to the orchestrations took place during rehearsals but nothing at that stage was likely to make the work any less baffling to its first audience. The reception was respectful, no more.

Back in New York, the Gatti-Casazza/Toscanini deal had been signed, Gatti-Casazza was installed as Director, and in line with everyone's worst fears, the Italian maestro had straightway insisted that he conduct *Tristan und Isolde* as the opening production of the new season on 16th November. In a letter to Andreas Dippel, Associate Director of the Met, Mahler was quite adamant.

'It is inconceivable to me that a new production of 'Tristan' should be put on without my being consulted in any way, and I cannot give my consent . . . If recently – out of consideration for the wishes of my colleague [Toscanini] – I gave a free hand to the new director, it was with the express exception of 'Tristan'. I took very special pains with 'Tristan' last season and can well maintain that the form in which this work now appears in New York is my spiritual property.'

Toscanini *did* open the season, but with *Aida*, not *Tristan* (Emmy Destinn in the title role and Caruso as 'Radames'). For the moment, anyway, a potentially explosive situation had been defused.

Mahler himself returned to the Met's podium the following January, 1909, with a newly staged production of Mozart's *Marriage of Figaro* and, in February, with the USA première of Smetana's *The Bartered Bride*. *Figaro* (miraculously honed by Mahler in a mere twenty rehearsals) was one significant success of his brief reign at the Met, but none was greater than his triumphant *Tristan und Isolde* – a year later on 12th March, 1910 : 'The stars were kind. I have never known a performance of *Tristan* to equal this' Mahler confided in Alma after the performance. It was another of those occasions where even the sceptics could do little but bow to his genius. The reviews were positively rhapsodic:

'There was an 'Isolde' last night [Fremstad] who may sometimes remember with a great glow of joy her performance of May 12th, 1909. A superb, a queenly tragic 'Isolde, this, but she was not alone in her glory . . . Mr. Mahler hurled all petty restraints to the four winds . . . and turned loose such a torrent of vital sound as he had never before let us hear . . . the crash of the death motive when 'Isolde' raised the cup to her lips was cataclysmic.'

Mahler never conducted *Tristan* again. Indeed, he only conducted one more opera at the Met: the American première of his old favourite from Vienna – Tchaikovsky's *Pique Dame* (Queen of Spades). In the cast – appropriately – was one of the most celebrated of his Vienna company: Leo Slezak, as 'Herman'.

New York's Manhattan skyline, 1908.

Most of the difficulties relating to Mahler's New York period came about as a direct result of his association with the Philharmonic – or rather the Philharmonic Society Committee. Otherwise he warmed very quickly to the city and its people. He felt welcomed by their unbridled, easy-going openness and strangely at home in what might just as easily have proved to be a forbidding environment after the elegant graces of Europe and, in particular, Vienna. The spectacular, futuristic beauty of the New York skyline intrigued him. He loved watching the teeming crowds on Fifth Avenue and became quite infatuated with the city subway which he rode at every opportunity rather than take taxis. Initially, on their first trip, he and Alma were housed in a lavish suite on the 11th floor of the Majestic Hotel overlooking Central Park. Later they inhabited the Savoy where most of the top Metropolitan artists stayed.

Mahler's first orchestral excursions in New York were with Walter Damrosch's 'Symphony Society': a series of three concerts during Novemer and December 1908, his second visit to the city. Mahler was not altogether thrilled by the general air of apathy in the orchestra (rehearsal attendances, for instance, were irregular and undisciplined) while press and audiences alike were certainly not accustomed to his brand of rugged, dramatic force in such works as Beethoven's Fifth Symphony. 'Rough handling' they called it. The last of these concerts featured the first American performance of his own Second Symphony and it was at the close of this particular evening (received, it seems, with a somewhat dutiful and disinterested response very much in line with the level of orchestral playing on this occasion) that Mahler was first approached by a female delegation from the Philharmonic Society. The Philharmonic's then self-governing orchestra had been in the doldrums for some time. Most of New York's finest players were now understandably being attracted by the greater security on offer to them from the three opera orchestras (the Met had created two orchestras to enable it to play in two cities on the same evening and thus out-trump Hammerstein's Manhattan Opera). So, in order to salvage themselves from a most precarious existence, the Philharmonic were now left with no alternative but to implement a system which would guarantee permanent engagements for their players under the directorship of a prestigious conductor. It would mean disbanding the co-operative scheme (and this was the beginning of the end for such a system in the USA) and installing an independent Board of Governors or Committee who would then, in theory, place absolute artistic control and authority in the hands of the chosen conductor. In practice, such was not to be the case as we shall see; however, a fund had been raised and the aforementioned ladies were now approaching Mahler to replace the current Principal Conductor, Vassily Safonoff, and train a completely new orchestra. As yet, they were too dazzled by Mahler's glowing pedigree to foresee how his uncompromising controversiality might possibly upset their apple-cart. Mahler, meanwhile, was clearly tempted by the challenge and, to their delight, he accepted.

The Society immediately set up two concerts in order to publicly display their prize aquisition. The programmes were fairly standard (31st March, 1909: Schumann's *Manfred* Overture, Beethoven's Seventh Symphony, Wagner's *Siegfried Idyll* and *Tannhäuser* Overture; 6th April: Beethoven's *Egmont* Overture and the Ninth Symphony), but the performances were far from routine. Generally the critics did their level best to acknowledge some renewal of energy and élan in the playing but, as one or two perceptive observers pointed out, there was no getting away from the fact that the quality of the orchestra was well below the standards to which Mahler rightly aspired and that clearly he would need to implement some very radical changes in the personnel for the following season. By all accounts the woodwind in particular made a shabby impression in both concerts.

Mahler and Alma retreated for the summer just after the Philharmonic débuts, stopping off for a time in Paris where Mahler made the acquaintance of the great French sculptor, Auguste Rodin, and sat for the famous bronze bust which now stands in the foyer of the Vienna State Opera. His mood had lightened, or rather grown more positive, during the first part of the year. The old determination had returned – or so a revealing letter to Bruno Walter suggested. Quite a contrast here to the letter that Walter received the previous summer:

I have lived through so much in the last year and a half. I can hardly talk

Auguste Rodin's famous bronze bust of Mahler.

about it. How should I attempt to describe so appalling a crisis! I see everything in a new light – feel so much alive, and the habit of being alive is sweeter than ever. I should not be surprised at times if suddenly I should notice that I had a new body (like Faust in the last scene) . . . How foolish it is . . . to be untrue even for a short hour to oneself and to higher things above us . . . Strange! When I hear music – even while I conduct – I can hear quite definite answers to all my questions and feel entirely clear and sure. Or rather, I feel quite clearly that they are not questions at all.

Doubtless this renewal of spirit was, for the most part, a conscious effort to counter the mounting oppression brought on by his physical condition. Alma, on the other hand, was clearly finding it an enormous strain living with these growing anxieties. By June of the summer her nerves were frayed to such an extent that it was thought best for both of them that she stay in Levico while he join friends at Göding near Toblach. It was here that he began work on the Ninth Symphony:

I feel marvellous here! To be able to sit working by the open window, and breathing the air, the trees and flowers all the time – this is a delight I have never known till now. I see now how perverse my life in summer has always been. I feel myself getting better every minute. I shudder when I think of my various 'workshops'; although I have spent the happiest hours of my life in them, it has probably been at the price of my health.

It says a great deal about Mahler's 'brave front' against fast diminishing odds that such pre-occupation with death, such bitter, restless undercurrents as his Ninth Symphony embodies, were in no way outwardly reflected at the time he set to work on it. As Deryck Cooke so aptly puts it, the Ninth is Mahler's

. . . dark night of the soul; and it is all the more moving in that there is no easy yielding to despair. Amid the heartache of the Finale, after all the horror and hopelessness of the first three movements, Mahler's unquenched love of life still shines through, thanks to the capacity of great music for expressing contrary feelings simultaneously. The symphony stands as a musical equivalent of the poet Rilke's 'dennoch preisen' – 'praising life in spite of everything'.

The sweet farewells of *Das Lied von der Erde* had far from quelled Mahler's innermost turmoil. Death permeates every fibre of the apocalyptic first movement of the Ninth – one of his very greatest achievements, both in the rarity of its vision and the prodigious inventiveness of the execution. A halting pulse, set out at the onset, immediately suggests his own erratic heartbeat. Ghostly flickers of colour from harp, muted horn and violas gradually transmute into a warm, singing melody on the violins, full of tender longing and vulnerable apprehension. But dark shadows again and again fall across its air of fulfilment. Moments of wonder, of jubilation even, are all too predictably beaten down by disfiguring bouts of despair, the third and greatest of these finally bringing the *certainty* of death in all its awsome power. Trombones and timpani hammer out the tolling harp figure from the opening of the movement '*mit hochster gewalt*' ('with the greatest force'), and from the menacing funeral-like procession which follows, struggles that beautiful D major melody again – hideously distorted.

The central movements are bitterness and dissollusionment run amok. Even the at first seemingly innocent little Ländler of the second movement quirkily reveals itself as something charmless, awkward and grotesque: 'The dance of life', as Mahler put it, turned sour and idiotic. The poisonous Rondo-Burleske which follows is ferocious and sacriligious: a contemptuous sneer at the futility of it all. Its fragmentation of thematic material is a classic example of techniques later picked up from Mahler and developed further by Webern and Berg. Mahler dedicated the movement to his 'brothers in Apollo', implying a sarcastic jibe at those who suggested that he could not write true counterpoint. The music fair blisters with jagged, disjointed counterpoints.

At last, the Finale courageously breaks in: and not a moment too soon. Ironically, its life-giving, hymn-like main theme is built out of transfigured fragments from the single moment of repose in the preceding Burleske movement. Now the music pours forth passionately, its progreess unimpeded. Eventually, after a truly heart-breaking climax – the brass there pealing out majestically in defiance – Mahler does at last find his oasis of peace and spiritual calm. Not that those dying strings phrases on which the Ninth ends can now be regarded as anything like his final words. The last pages of Deryck Cooke's performing version of the unfinished Tenth reveal otherwise.

The remaining summer months passed and the autumn approached in a climate of relative optimism. Before setting sail for New York again in October, Mahler renewed his happy association with the Concertgebouw Orchestra for performances of the Seventh Symphony. With the tentative insecurities of the New York orchestra still lingering in his mind, music-making of this calibre was balm indeed.

Back in New York, however, the promised restorations on the Philharmonic were well underway in preparation for the opening of the 68th Season on 4th November. There was a new Concert Master, Theodore Spiering, changes for the better had been made in the woodwind personnel, and more workable proportions arrived at in the strings; the number of basses, for instance, had been reduced from fourteen to eight. As regards concert planning, a number of major new projects were mooted to supplement the

125

regular Thursday evening and Friday afternoon dates (these were the early days of the subscription system; repeat performances of the same programme meant more time available for rehearsal). A trial series of Sunday afternoon concerts was launched, a complete cycle of the Beethoven symphonies, a novelty series of 'historical' concerts covering ground onwards from Bach (Handel, Rameau, Gretry and Haydn were among those featured), a special series to take place at the Brooklyn Academy, and the orchestra's first tour – to New Haven, Springfield, Providence, Philadelphia and Boston (and Mahler insisted, contrary to general custom at the time, that the orchestra would tour at full strength).

Clearly the Philharmonic Society, now under the jurisdiction of their awesome women's committee led by one, Mrs. Sheldon, were determined to build up the prestige of their orchestra so that it might vie for a position of superiority with the most celebrated of its rivals: the Boston Symphony. And what better opportunity than this. No conductor at the time was better equipped to co-ordinate the orchestra's technical skills than Mahler, nor was anyone more likely to fire its enthusiasm with such individual interpretative flair. Who, for instance, could lay claim to so instinctive a sense of the underlying thinking behind a Beethoven score, regardless of any surface liberties he may have taken?

Well, unfortunately, it was very soon plain that New York's traditionalists were no different to their opposite numbers in Vienna. Accustomed as they were to the cool classicism favoured by the majority of Mahler's predecessors, it would take time for them to adjust – if indeed they were to adjust at all – to so impassioned an approach to music-making as Mahler fostered.

New York equivalents of Vienna's most carping critics quickly emerged from the woodwork. Henry E. Krehbiel of the New York Tribune, first chronicler and programme annotator for the Philharmonic objected most strongly to Mahler's doubling of wind voices and other minor adjustments in the Beethoven symphonies. He took issue, for example, over the addition of a second timpanist for 'The Storm' in the 'Pastoral' symphony and the insertion of an Eb clarinet into the finale of the 'Eroica'. On this point, Mahler argued that since the tune in question was of the raucous, hungarian variety, Beethoven too would surely have heightened its 'gypsy music' effect in this way had the instrument been available to him. Again he reiterated the belief that he had put forward time and again in Vienna: that no composer should regard his work as sacrosanct if genuine improvements to its clarity or character later became feasible through technical advancement. It was still a dangerous, even arrogant argument to pursue, but it grew far less defensible where the composer in question was still around to make the changes for himself if he so chose. Richard Strauss was a prime instance. Mahler made fairly hefty instrumental additions to the scoring of *Don Juan* on the premise that Strauss was a young man when he completed it and would no doubt have thought differently by then. Similarly, in *Till Eulenspiegel*, the prankster Till's last strangulated cries of protest as he faces the hangman's noose were always transposed from a high D clarinet to an ordinary clarinet in a Mahler performance – an idea which certainly intensified the moment, since it was nigh on impossible to play, on an ordinary clarinet, what Strauss had written on the stave, without a desperate squawk issuing forth. Exactly how Strauss reacted to these changes, if indeed he did not give his approval, remains largely speculative.

Interestingly enough, Mahler's own music actually went down better in New York than some of his more unorthodox handling of familiar fare. The aforementioned Krehbiel, however, was one of those who did not even begin to appreciate its crucial juxtaposition of lyrical beauty and crass ugliness:

There is no reason why Mahler should be a prophet of the ugly, as he discloses himself in the last movement of the Symphony in D. He makes that plain by interrupting a painfully cacophonous din with an episode built on a melody which is exquisitely lovely and profoundly moving.

New York 'World', 16th December, 1909.

It was in the light of such disturbingly naïve remarks that Mahler took the unprecedented step of forbidding Krehbiel – arch-guardian of New York's musical standards – to provide notes for his (Mahler's) symphonies. In the event, only the First, Second and Fourth were ever performed there.

Most commentators on Mahler's brief period with the New York Philharmonic are apt to stress its general failure, yet one should at least acknowledge that in the space of only two seasons the orchestra's repertoire had already begun to expand – albeit very gradually – into a number of fascinating new areas. One or two contemporary American composers had crept into the programming: Edward MacDowell, for instance, was represented by his D minor Piano Concerto; works by Chadwick, Hadley and Loeffler also appeared, and – astonishingly – Mahler even had plans to include one of the Charles Ives' symphonies in the third season that he was never able to bring to fruition.

One area in which he clearly felt a certain affinity was French music. He had already expressed his approval of the innovative Berlioz *Symphonie Fantastique* back in Vienna, and sure enough, it appeared once again as the showpiece at the centre of the Philharmonic's first tour. Dukas' *Sorcerer's Apprentice*, Bizet's first *L'Arlesienne* Suite (with chorus), Chabrier's *Espagna*, Debussy's *Nocturnes* and the two completed movements of his *Images – Rondes*

Edward Elgar.

*du Printemps* and *Iberia* – and works by Massenet and Lalo also featured during the course of some forty programmes that he conducted during the 1910 – 1911 season.

There was English music too. Elgar's *Sea Pictures* (exluding *The Swimmer*. Solioist: Kirkby-Lunn) and *Enigma Variations*, and, on less familiar ground, Sir Charles Stanford's *Irish Symphony*: a curious choice given the potential English repertoire open to him. One wonders, for instance, what he would have made of the Elgar Symphonies or, perhaps more appropriately, Elgar's Concert Overture *In the South* – the composer at his most Straussian.

Doubtless Mahler's programmes would have grown progressively more ambitious had his time in New York been longer and had the Philharmonic committee adopted a more enterprising and encouraging stand. As it was, one can see how his choice was largely governed by the training requirements of the orchestra, to say nothing of a general reluctance on the part of his audiences to accept experiment. The average New Yorkers were apt to stay away in droves when anything of a remotely contemporary nature was billed on the schedules; hardly surprising given the discouraging noises from the press every time anyone showed signs of enterprise. Mahler's predecessor, Vassily Safonoff, was heavily criticised for attempting to liven up Philharmonic programmes by introducing a younger breed of Russian composer to New York audiences – Scriabin being the most notable example.

128

Sergei Rachmaninov.

The mainstay, then, of Mahler's New York programmes was the traditional German repertoire – Mozart, Beethoven and Wagner – but to this he did manage to add a number of Strauss works – *Ein Heldenleben* and *Also Sprach Zarathustra* as well as *Don Juan* and *Till Eulenspiegel* already mentioned – and the occasional rarity such as Hans Pfitzner's little-known Overture, *Christelflein*. Incidently, Alma insists that Mahler conducted all Bruckner's symphonies whilst in New York. This, as others have pointed out, is simply not true. In fact, he conducted only the Fourth during his stay. Bruckner was anyway not without his champions in the United States at the time.

By all accounts, it seems that the highlights of Mahler's two seasons with the Philharmonic centred around his collaborations with a number of legendary soloists: Kreisler gave the Brahms and Beethoven Violin Concertos, Joseph Lhevinne, the Tchaikovsky First Piano Concerto, and, perhaps most memorable of all, Rachmaninov in his own Third Piano Concerto on 16th January, 1910. At the time, Rachmaninov was none too enamoured with business-minded American attitudes to music-making and Mahler, for him, exuded all the thoroughness and committment that he found so lacking elsewhere:

Mahler was the only conductor whom I considered worthy to be classed with Nikisch. He devoted himself to the concerto until the

129

Ferruccio Busoni.

accompaniment, which is rather complicated, had been practised to perfection . . . According to Mahler, every detail of the score was important – an attitude too rare among conductors.

Unquestionably, the most significant and durable of all Mahler's musical partnerships in New York, though, was that which grew between him and the Italian pianist and composer, Ferruccio Busoni. Both men had tremendous professional and personal admiration for one another. 'Being with you has a sort of purifying effect', Busoni once said of working with Mahler. 'One only has to come near you to feel young again'.

Mahler conducted two of Busoni's own works whilst in New York (the *Turandot* Suite and the première of his *Berceuse Élégiaque*) but it was their memorable concerto collaborations which truly established the bonds between them ('With what love and unerring instinct this man rehearsed!' wrote Busoni to his wife on one occasion). Of course, the marrying of two such strongly individual temperaments was bound to produce work which would irritate the purists: and sure enough, it did. Their extrovert, but life-enhancing reading of Beethoven's 'Emperor' Concerto was such as to prompt a tearful 'visitation' from Mrs. Sheldon and her 'watch' committee: 'No Mr. Mahler, this will never do', came the indignant verdict following one of the rehearsals.

By now Mahler must have realised how little room there was for artistic manoeuvering within the confines imposed by the Philharmonic Society Committee. The arrogance of these 'simple wealthy ladies' (as Richard Schickel describes them in his book, 'The World of Carnegie Hall') was astonishing. They had, as Schickel goes on, 'little knowledge of music and no love for it . . . [they] were simply not the people to deal with such a temperament [Mahler's]. For them music was merely a pleasurable activity, in a category with charity balls and shopping expeditions'. Yet they would think nothing of pitting their untrained ears against one of the foremost Beethoven interpreters of his time. Mahler was dumbfounded. As Alma later recalled: 'To his amazement he had ten women ordering him about like a puppet'. Any former commitment that artistic policy would rest firmly in the hands of the prinicpal conductor was plainly not about to be honoured, and since it pained the committee that Mahler would not bend to their influence, as had clearly been intended, their petty, interfering demands grew more insistant. Every time he doubled the wind in a Beethoven symphony, every time a 'non-commercial' work appeared on a Philharmonic programme, our disillusioned ladies would bear down on him.

In the middle of February 1911, Mahler was finally summoned before the full committee and soundly reprimanded for a number of supposed transgressions. Severe restrictions on his powers – restrictions that had, in effect, been deceitfully, though not officially, imposed from the very start – were now formally enforced. It must have been a belittling spectacle: a musician of Mahler's stature forced into defending his artistic policy to a motley group of New York spinsters. Humiliated and infuriated, he stormed out, knowing full well that here was an end to any ambitions he might have had for the Philharmonic.

Not all the Philharmonic players 'hated' Mahler, as Alma has said. His working methods inevitably aroused some antagonism and dislike, just as they had done in Vienna, but, as one of the New York violinists, Herman Martonne, put it:

If you did your duty and did it well and did it with your heart, then he had nothing against you. I was shocked sometimes at how he jumped at people and fixed-up scores, but for inner sensitivity, atmosphere – as a musician – gigantic.

These, and a number of other New York players' recollections originate from a series of taped interviews commercially issued on gramophone record for a time as a bonus to Leonard Bernstein's recording of the Sixth Symphony with the New York Philharmonic. They make riveting listening, not least for the revealing way in which they put into perspective some of the distortions that have been handed down since then relating to Mahler's relationship with his players.

According to one or two of these survivors, the temperament and the tantrums were very much a part of the intense atmosphere that he found it necessary to generate whilst making music. One player recalls an almost exact parallel to the incident in Vienna when he tore relentlessly into the orchestra over the opening of Beethoven's Fifth Symphony. 'We never could give him enough volume', said the player relating the episode, but when he had finally achieved the intensity of sound that he had been after, he was so delighted that he invited the whole orchestra to take a snack with him in order that everyone should share in the excitement of what they – collectively – had accomplished.

Most players seem to agree that Mahler's actual beat was appallingly difficult to follow. By the time he arrived in New York, his technique had anyway mellowed somewhat from the demonstrative extremes of his early days in Europe. He now relied upon a more inward communication with his players conveyed only through the expressiveness of his hands and eyes, and of course, the intangible aura of his presence. Players recall how he favoured a pliable approach to tempi and phrasing ('the difference between freedom and slavery' was how one player put it: others thought it more excessive) and encouraged a liberal use of portamento (sliding between notes) and vibrato in keeping with the typically Viennese brand of string playing that he was so slavishly trying to instil into his New York Players.

'He made us sing the music just as he did', commented one player demonstrating exactly how Mahler would sing to the orchestra in order to illustrate the precise phrasing he was after.

Comparisons inevitably arose with Toscanini, of course, though in retrospect few of the orchestra, it seems, had any doubts as to where the more profound musicianship lay. Another player, Herbert Borodkin, very effectively managed to crystallise the essential differences between them. For him, Toscanini always remained Toscanini, whereas Mahler entered into the spirit of every composer he conducted. The 'inner sensitivity' that Herman Martonne talked of was the key to his intuitively being able to capture the essence of what each composer was trying to say. In the end, the notes themselves became superfluous. Asked one day if he could make his beat clearer, Mahler replied, 'Good players don't need a conductor. The conductor is a necessary evil!' A strange comment, one might think, coming from one whose podium authoritarianism was second to none. Yet it is not hard to see what he meant. Coaxing or cajoling orchestras into sharing his conception in order that they should be as one, was primarily a phsychological process in which practical technicalities were invariably a hindrance. Mahler actually resented having to tell players how to shape or colour a phrase which is perhaps why he tended to over-react when it became necessary to do so. Like all precocious geniuses, he never could understand those who did not automatically share his vision, be it a single phrase, a movement, or an entire symphony.

Mahler conducted his last concert with the Philharmonic on 21st February, 1911, only days before his upsetting showdown with the committee. His toxic throat condition had flared up again, and strictly against all medical advice but as a gesture of loyalty to his friend Busoni whose 'Berceuse Élégiaque' was being premièred that evening, he rose from his sick-bed in order to be there. It was an all-Italian programme – works by Sinigaglia, Martucci and Bossi. Toscanini was in the audience.

According to Alma, Mahler's worsening health brought out the best in the American goodwill and generosity, but it provided too a golden opportunity for the Philharmonic committee to ease a replacement into Mahler's position. Joseph Stransky became the eventual choice as permanent Music Director, but for the remaining concerts of that season the leader, Theodore Spiering, took over. In a virtual replica of Mahler's Vienna betrayal, a predictable chorus of acclaim for Spiering went up from Mahler's opposition. Busoni was there to witness the sorry scenes:

The behaviour of the New York audience and the critics over the matter will remain in my memory as one of my most painful experiences. The sensation made by a leader of an orchestra being able to conduct unprepared has made a greater impression on them than Mahler's whole personality was ever able to do! Spiering has been exalted to the position of one of the greatest conductors, and they have spoken quite seriously about his continuing to fill the post. *Not one word of regret has fallen about Mahler's absence!* One reads of such things happening in history, but when it is a personal experience, one is filled with despair".

A letter from Busoni to his wife on 30th March, 1911.

When the Philharmonic came to stage their memorial concert to Mahler on 23rd November, 1911, his genius as a composer was represented by just one fragment of his music: the first movement of the Fifth Symphony. In due course they would come to mourn their neglect, but for the time being, this alone was New York's tribute.

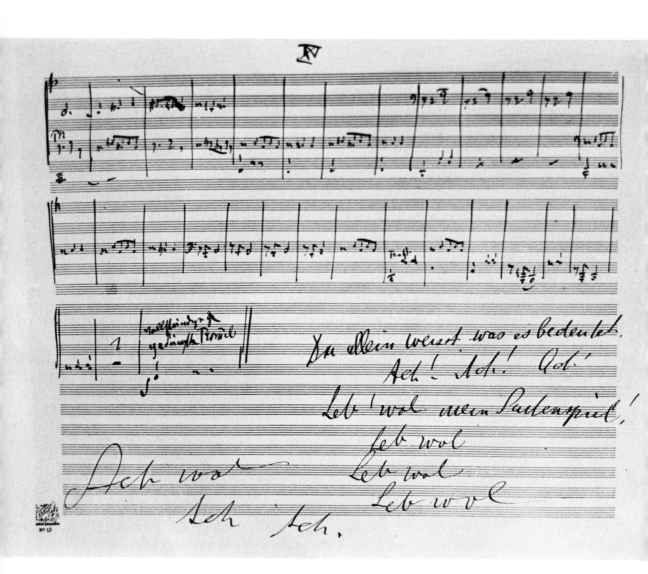

# 10. 'To live for you! To die for you! Almschi!'

Scrawled across the manuscripts of Mahler's unfinished Tenth Symphony are the tell-tale exclamations of a soul in torment: 'Mercy! . . . Oh God! Oh God! Why hast thou forsaken me? . . . You alone know what it means . . . Farewell my lyre!' On the final page of all, the words 'To live for you! To die for you! Almschi!' impart an unbearable poignancy; the handwriting here is huge, shaky, almost uncontrolled in its emotion.

In these impromptu scribblings lies the key to Mahler's distraught frame of mind during the last year of his life, for each painful word is clearly addressed to the one he could not bear to lose but now feared he might – Alma.

By the summer of 1910, Mahler's marriage was teetering ever more precariously. Alma had never been quite the same since the dreadful month of July 1907, but Mahler's deteriorating health and restrictive physical regime were clearly making matters worse. So close was she now, in fact, to a nervous breakdown, that an immediate rest cure under proper medical supervision was seen as the only possible solution. In May she entered the sanitorium at Tobeldad and there began a curiously fateful course of treatment. Worried by her despondency, one of the doctors prescribed dancing in the hope that such a diversion might help to lighten her mood. In the event, however, his therapy did more than lighten her mood, for it was during one of these sessions that she made the aquantance of Walter Gropius: a handsome young architect, four years her junior.

Alma was never so ripe for the attentions of another as she was now. Plainly her marriage to Mahler had never fully satisfied certain of her physical needs. Some have suggested that Mahler was struck by intermittent impotency; others, more logically I think, that his sexual drive was never very strong and that he sublimated almost exclusively through his creative pursuits. Whatever the truth, one could scarcely blame Alma (by her own admission, highly sexed) for succumbing to temptation from elsewhere. She was, after all, an immensely attractive and alluring young woman.

No sooner had she and Gropius met when he declared his love for her. She should leave Mahler and go to him, he implored in a letter

End of the Fourth Movement from the facsimile edition of the Tenth Symphony, Vienna 1924.

135

Walter Gropius.

impatiently written shortly after she had returned to Toblach. By accident, however (or so he somewhat dubiously maintained later) Gropius had addressed the letter to 'Herr Direktor Mahler'. The whole issue was suddenly out in the open. In the emotional scenes which followed Mahler summoned Gropius to the house and insisted that Alma make a choice. In spite of all, nobody knew better than she that there was simply no choice to be made.

I could never have imagined life without him . . . least of all could I have imagined life with another man. I had often thought of going away somewhere alone to start life afresh, but never with any thought of another person. Mahler was the hub of my existence.

Once and for all, the grievances that she had resentfully harboured within herself for far too long were put before her husband. Mahler was prostrate. Guilt overwhelmed him. He even consulted Sigmund Freud – a famous encounter, though more revealing of Mahler's psyche, it seems, than it was helpful to him; he became as submissive and caring overnight as he had been blindly inconsiderate before. 'Almschi', he wrote some weeks later, 'if you had left me that time, I should simply have gone out like a torch deprived of air'. Suddenly she was the focus of his every breath. He placed notes by her bed while she slept, and in one gesture of belated remorse insisted that all her early compositions, forcibly put aside at his behest, should be revised and reconsidered.

136

The realisation that he may have stifled her creative urges had all at once dawned on him. It was as if he were waking from a very long dream.

Just as the Tenth Symphony was riddled with the insecurity of losing Alma, so the forthcoming première of the mighty Eighth Symphony in Munich stood as a monument to his undying love. 'Does it not make the impression of a betrothal?' was how he offered the dedication to her. Love letters streamed from his pen during the rehearsal period, the last reading thus:

For the first time for eight weeks – in my whole life, for that matter – I feel the blissful happiness love gives to one who, loving with all his soul, knows he is loved in return. After all, my dream has come true: 'I lost the world, but found my harbour!'

A few days before the scheduled performances in Munich's massive Exhibition Hall (12th and 13th September), Mahler's septic throat infection struck yet again. Only willpower fortified him to overcome a high temperature in time for the final rehearsal: 'Every note addressed to you' were his parting words to Alma. The array of performers assembled for the occasion was staggering. The

A rehearsal prior to the first performance of the Eighth Symphony in Munich.

augmented orchestra of the Munich Concert Society alone comprised 84 strings, 2 harps, 22 woodwind, and 17 brass, plus the 4 trumpets and 3 trombones set apart from the main body of the orchestra. A total of 171 instrumentalists. The vocal contingent of 858 singers was composed of 250 members of the Singverein of the Gesellschaft der Musikfreunde (Vienna); 250 members of the Riedel Verein (Leipzig); 350 children from the Zentral Singschule (Munich), and 8 soloists (from Berlin, Frankfurt, Hamburg, Munich, Vienna and Wiesbaden).

Mahler would never conduct in Europe again. But then nothing could easily have surpassed the triumph of this unforgettable occasion: a fitting climax to a lifetime's devoted endeavour. Alma and Bruno Walter were, of course, both present:

The entire audience rose to their feet as soon as Mahler took his place at the conductor's desk; and the breathless silence which followed was the most impressive homage an artist could be paid . . . And then, Mahler, god or demon, turned those tremendous volumes of sound into fountains of light. The experience was indescribable. Incredible, too, was the demonstration that followed. The whole audience surged towards the platform and gave Mahler a 30 minute ovation.

Alma, in 'Memories and Letters'.

The huge apparatus devotedly obeyed the word and the master's hand that ruled it without effort. All the performers were in a state of solemn exaltation, most of all perhaps the children, whose hearts had belonged to him from the beginning. What a moment when, to the applause of thousands of listeners in the gigantic Exhibition Hall, he took his place before the thousand performers – at a climax of his life and already marked out by fate for an early death – when his work now called on the *creator spiritus,* from whose fire it had been created within him, when from every lip the cry of yearning of his life was heard: *accende lumen sensibus infunde amorem cordibus!* When the last note of the performance had died away and the storm of enthusiasm roared out to him Mahler climbed the steps of the platform, at the top of which the children's chorus was stationed, cheering with all their might, and he shook every hand that was held out to him, walking right along the row.

Bruno Walter, *Gustav Mahler.*

The final phase of Mahler's life, painful to relate, was mercifully brief.

Back in New York the ever more virulent throat infection finally forced him to abandon the last part of his Philharmonic season. Joseph Frankel, his New York doctor, took blood tests in order to confirm the diagnosis of acute streptococcal infection and having done so, urged Mahler to consult a bacterialogical expert in Paris – then the centre for bacterial studies following Pasteur's discoveries. André Chantemesse of the Pasteur Institute was disconcertingly enthusiastic about Mahler's splendidly developed

138

The last picture of Mahler, on board ship during his final crossing to Europe in the spring of 1911.

streptococci – among the finest specimens that he had encountered – but, as yet, could offer no remedy.

Mahler's condition fluctuated now between sporadic rallying and sudden relapse. Alma recalls the astounding transformation that took place in him when they arrived in Paris. It was as if Europe were indeed having the restorative effect that he always maintained it would. He dressed and shaved himself, remarked on being hungry, and asked to be taken for a drive through Paris. 'He got into the car as a man recovered', wrote Alma, 'and got out of it as a man at death's door'.

From this point on, his condition worsened dramatically. As a last resort Alma sent for Professor Franz Chvostek, a famous blood specialist from the Vienna Medical School. He offered no hope but suggested that, psychologically, Mahler might be happier if he were moved back to Vienna.

Vienna – the hub of his greatest ambitions and scene of so many triumphs, trials and tribulations – the only musical home that he had ever known. Flowers and cards filled his room at the Löw Sanitorium. Friends surrounded him: Arnold Berliner, Bruno

139

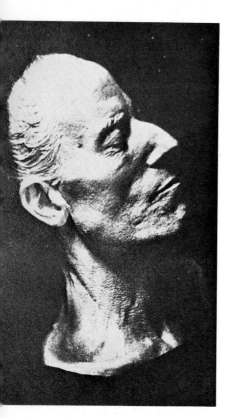

Mahler's death mask taken by Carl Moll.

Walter: 'There he lay, tortured victim of an insidious illness, his very soul affected by the struggle of his body, his mood gloomy and forbidding', wrote Walter. Mahler was anxious to hear about all his old friends; he expressed concern about what was to become of Arnold Schoenberg and still found the strength to grouse about current policies at the State Opera. To Alma he entrusted the sketches of his Tenth Symphony which had not been touched since his arrival in Paris. Through this gesture alone he had fully resigned himself.

His awareness faded now. He even failed to recognise his own sister Justine who fled the room in despair. Gradually he sank deeper into coma. Only Alma's name lingered on his lips now. 'My Almschi', he repeated again and again.

Shortly after 11 o'clock on the evening of 18th May, 1911, Mahler died. Like Beethoven, he passed on amidst the fury of a thunderstorm. His last word: 'Mozart'.

In keeping with his own wishes, he was buried in the churchyard at Grinzing, Vienna, in the same grave as his elder daughter, 'Putzi'. The headstone, he asked, should bear only one word: MAHLER. 'Anyone who comes to look for me will know who I was and the rest do not need to know'.

Bruno Walter was one of a few selected friends at the simple ceremony on 19th May:

As we laid the coffin in the cemetary at Grinzing, a storm broke and such torrents of rain fell that it was almost impossible to proceed. A immense crowd, dead silent, followed the hearse. At the moment when the coffin was lowered, the sun broke through the clouds'.

The story does not quite end there. Six months after Mahler's death, Bruno Walter posthumously premièred *Das Lied von der Erde* in Munich. Seven months later, he conducted the first performance of the Ninth Symphony in Vienna. Mahler's symphonic canon was complete, the catalogue closed; or so it seemed.

In 1912, Arnold Schoenberg wrote:

We shall know as little about what [Mahler's] Tenth (for which, as also in the case of Beethoven, sketches exist) would have said as we know about Beethoven's or Bruckner's. It seems that the Ninth is a limit. He who wants to go beyond it must pass away. It seems as if something might be imparted to us in the Tenth which we ought not yet to know, for we are not yet ready. Those who have written a Ninth stood too near to the hearafter. Perhaps the riddles of this world would be solved if one of those who knew them were to write a Tenth. And that probably is not to take place.

140

Mahler's grave in the
Grinzing cemetery.

In fact, when he wrote these words, Schoenberg, like many others, had no idea just how far Mahler had actually progressed on the Tenth. The sketches were still in Alma's over-protective possession and only she was fully aware of their true extent. In 1924, she finally asked the 23 year old composer, Ernst Krenek, then just married to Mahler's daughter Anna, to 'complete' the work. The idea of a 'performing' version such as Deryck Cooke later prepared, had simply not been considered at that stage and upon perusal of the sketches, Krenek deemed the task an obvious impossibility. The outcome, however, was his practical full score of the two most nearly complete movements: the opening Adagio and the strange little 'Purgatorio' movement with its ghostly ostinato echoes of the *Knaben Wunderhorn* song, *Das Iridische Leben* (Early Life). Needless to say, this curious pairing made little musical sense out of context.

Thereafter, the history of the Tenth grew into an international issue. Alma was persuaded by Mahler biographer Richard Specht to permit publication of a substantial part of the manuscript in facsimile and Specht, upon study of it, realised that far from being a closed book it would indeed be possible for 'some musician of high standing, devoted to Mahler and intimate with his style', to prepare a performable full score of the entire work. Arnold Schoenberg was approached, as was Dmitri Shostakovich in Russia. Both, for differing reasons, declined. Meanwhile, in England, Deryck Cooke, on the music staff of the BBC at the time, was in the throes of preparing a booklet to accompany their proposed Mahler Centenary celebrations in 1960. In order to 'flesh out' his comments on the Tenth, he immersed himself in a detailed study of the facsimile only to find that Mahler had in fact left not a 'might-have-been' but an 'almost-is'. 'The leading thematic line throughout', wrote Cooke, 'and something like 90% of the counterpoint and harmony are pure Mahler, and vintage Mahler at that'.

Cooke's first version, with both scherzos still incomplete, was broadcast by the BBC on 19th December 1960. The Philharmonia Orchestra was conducted by Berthold Goldschmidt.

There then followed something of a hiatus. Alma Mahler-Werfel – as she now was – influenced by Bruno Walter, decided to forbid further performances of Cooke's score even though neither she or Walter had seen or heard a note of it. It was not, then, until after Walter's death in 1962 that another conductor, Harold Byms, persuaded Alma to listen to a tape of Goldschmidt's 1960 performance. Cooke writes that she 'was moved to tears by the music, and confessed that she had not realised "how much Mahler there was in it".' On 8th May, 1963, she granted Cooke and the BBC permission for 'performances in any part of the world'. The

141

complete version was introduced at a promenade concert in the Royal Albert Hall, London, on 13th August, 1964 by Goldschmidt and the London Symphony Orchestra.

Many distinguished names since Bruno Walter have voiced their disapproval of Cooke's 'complete' Mahler Tenth – among them, Leonard Bernstein, Rafael Kubelik, Pierre Boulez and Carlo Maria Giulini. Yet, as Cooke himself pointed out, his score was 'in no sense intended as a "completion" or reconstruction . . . Quite simply, [it represents] the stage the work had reached when Mahler died, in a practical performing version'; and, as such, a revealing glimpse ahead to the beginnings of what was, after all, an enriching new phase in his creative development. As Cooke goes on, 'it shows clearly that Mahler, far from plunging further into pre-occupation with death, was moving towards a more vitally creative attitude'. The two scherzos, for instance, are informed with an exuberance and life-assertive energy that betray an entirely new kind of Mahler. Moreover, in no other symphony are the influences that he would exert on so much 20th century music more graphically anticipated: Alban Berg, in particular, and Hindemith, Shostakovich and Britten.

We would, then, be poorer in our perception and appreciation of Mahler's life-work had the Tenth been witheld from us. Doubtless, Mahler would, again in Cooke's words, have 'elaborated, refined and perfected . . . in a thousand details', but as it is, we can at least share in the enriching experience that it offers and contemplate, too, what might have been. After all, as Cooke so rightly said: 'There was still plenty of life left in Mahler when death claimed him: the Tenth Symphony reveals that the Ninth had been a phase, like the Sixth, which he had faced and overcome'.

To appreciate these words one has only to look at the last movement. A fearsome fortissimo thud on muffled bass drum, which seconds before had abruptly cut off the fourth movement scherzo, has the first word. Bass tuba and horns intensify the despairing gloom. The premonition of death hangs heavily. 'Du allein weisst was es bedeutet' ('You alone know what it means') wrote Mahler on the score at this point – one of the cryptic, soul-searching messages to Alma referred to earlier. She was to reveal its secret in her 'Memories and Letters':

Marie Uchatius, a young art student, paid me a visit one day in the Hotel Majestic. Hearing a confused noise, we leaned out of the window and saw a long procession in the broad street along the side of Central park. It was the funeral cortège of a fireman, of whose heroic death we had read in the newspaper. The chief mourners were almost immediately beneath us when the procession halted, and the master of ceremonies stepped forward and gave a short address. From our eleventh-floor window we could only guess what he said. There was a brief pause and then a stroke on the muffled drum, followed by a dead silence. The procession then moved forward and all was over.

The scene brought tears to our eyes and I looked anxiously at Mahler's window. But he too was leaning out and his face was streaming with tears. The brief drum-stroke impressed him so deeply that he used it in the Tenth Symphony.

Indeed, six times this ominous death-knell sounds before finally being silenced by a return of the awesome climax from the first movement Adagio: a terrifying nine-note dissonance from the entire orchestra which desperately attempts to stifle a sustained high A scream on the trumpet. Poignantly, the horns now reiterate the spare viola melody on which work opened, and the music moves into a rapturous postlude, at once ardent and serene. In Michael Kennedy's words: 'a great song of life and love – the most fervently intense ending to any Mahler symphony and a triumphant vindication of his spiritual courage'.

Here, then, lies the Tenth Symphony's true revelation. Far from looking back in peaceful, if regretful, resignation, as do both *Das Lied von der Erdé* and the Ninth Symphony, these closing pages stand squarely before the future, brimful of hope and new-found determination. For Mahler – ever the progressive spirit – there could be no more fitting epitaph.

The supreme value of Mahler's creative work does not lie in the newness which is so movingly revealed in the essential elements of a . . . daring, adventurous and bizarre character, but in the fact that this newness with its added . . . beauty, inspiration and soulfulness, has become music, and that the lasting values of artistic power and eminent humanity are at the bottom of these creations. This is why they have preserved their full vitality to this day . . . and will maintain it into the future.

Bruno Walter, *Gustav Mahler.*

143

# A Select Discography

The following discography is a personal, though I hope thoroughly objective, choice from the extensive selection of Mahler recordings now available to the record collector. Where I have found it difficult to choose between a group of particularly outstanding performances – each, perhaps, of widely differing merits – I have listed each of the records concerned. Availability in England, of course, is subject to change.

| | |
|---|---|
| *Symphony No. 1* | London Philharmonic Orchestra |
| | Klaus Tennstedt      HMV ASD 3541 |
| | London Symphony Orchestra |
| | James Levine      RCA ARL 10894 |
| | Columbia Symphony Orchestra |
| | Bruno Walter      CBS 61116 |
| | |
| *Symphony No. 2*<br>('Resurrection') | Chicago Symphony Orchestra & Chorus<br>Neblett/Horne/Claudio Abbado.<br>     DG 2707 094 (2 records)<br>London Philharmonic Orchestra & Chorus<br>Soffel/Mathis/Klaus Tennstedt<br>     Number not yet available<br>Philharmonia Orchestra & Chorus<br>Schwarzkopf/Rossl-Majdan/Otto<br>Klemperer      HMV SLS 806 (2 records)<br>New York Philharmonic Orchestra &<br>Chorus<br>Cundari/Forrester/Bruno Walter.<br>     CBS 61282/3 |
| | |
| *Symphony No. 3* | London Philharmonic Orchestra & Choir<br>Wenkel/Klaus Tennstedt<br>     HMV Digital SLS 5195 (2 records) |

London Symphony Orchestra
Ambrosian Singers/Procter/Jascha
Horenstein            Unicorn RHS 302/3
New York Philharmonic Orchestra &
Chorus
Lipton/Leonard Bernstein
                        CBS 77206 (2 records)

*Symphony No. 4*      Cleveland Orchestra
                      Raskin/George Szell      CBS 61056
                      Israel Philharmonic Orchestra
                      Hendricks/Zubin Mehta
                              Decca Digital SXDL 7501

*Symphony No. 5+*     New Philharmonia Orchestra
Ruckert Lieder        Janet Baker/Sir John Barbirolli
                      HMV SLS 785            (2 records)

*Symphony No. 5+*     Philadelphia Orchestra
Adagio from           James Levine
Symphony No. 10               RCA RL 02905 (2 records)

*Symphony No. 6*      Chicago Symphony Orchestra
                      Claudio Abbado
                              DG 2707 117 (2 records)
                      Berlin Philharmonic Orchestra
                      Herbert von Karajan
                              DG 2707 106 (2 records)

*Symphony No. 7*      London Philharmonic Orchestra
                      Klaus Tennstedt
                      HMV Digital SLS 5238      (2 records)

*Symphony No. 8*      Chicago Symphony Orchestra/Vienna
                      Opera & Vienna Boys Choirs
                      Harper/Popp/Auger/Minton/Watts/Kollo
                      Shirley-Quirk/Talvela/Sir Georg Solti
                              Decca SET 534/5.

*Symphony No. 9*      New Philharmonia Orchestra
                      Otto Klemperer
                      HMV Concert Classics SXDW 3021 (2
                                          records)
                      Berlin Philharmonic Orchestra
                      Herbert von Karajan
                              DG 2707 125 (2 records)

| | |
|---|---|
| *Symphony No. 10*<br>Deryck Cooke<br>performing version | Bournemouth Symphony Orchestra<br>Simon Rattle<br>   HMV Digital SLS 5206 (2 records) |
| *Das Lied von der Erde* | Christa Ludwig/Fritz Wunderlich<br>Philharmonia Orchestra/Otto Klemperer<br>   HMV SAN 179<br>Dietrich Fischer-Dieskau/James King/<br>Vienna Philharmonic Orchestra/Leonard<br>Bernstein   Decca Jubilee JB 13 |
| *Das Klagende Lied* | Concertgebouw Orchestra/Netherlands<br>Radio Choir/Harper/Proctor/Hollweg/<br>Bernard Haitink   Philips 6500 587 |
| *Kindertotenlieder*<br>(+ Adagio from<br>Symphony No. 10 | Janet Baker/Israel Philharmonic Orchestra<br>Leonard Bernstein   CBS 76475 |
| *Lieder aus Des<br>Knaben Wunderhorn* | Elisabeth Schwarzkopf/Dietrich Fischer-<br>Dieskau/London Symphony Orchestra<br>George Szell   HMV SAN 218 |
| *Lieder eines Fahrenden<br>Gessellen* | Fischer-Dieskau/Bavarian Radio<br>Symphony Orchestra/Rafael Kubelik<br>(with Symphony No. 5)<br>   DG 2726 064 (2 records)<br>Mildred Miller/Columbia Symphony<br>Orchestra/Bruno Walter<br>   (with Symphony No. 9) CBS 61369/70 |
| *Ruckert Lieder*<br>(see Symphony No. 5) | |
| *Lieder und Gesange<br>aus der Jugendzeit* | Dietrich Fischer-Dieskau/Daniel<br>Barenboim<br>(with collection of songs)<br>   HMV SLS 5173 (3 records) |

# Selected Bibliography

ADLER, Guido: *Gustav Mahler* (Universal Edition, Vienna 1911-16)

BAUER-LECHNER, Natalie: *Recollections of Gustav Mahler* (Trans. Dika Newlin. Ed. Peter Franklin; Faber, London 1980)

BLAUKOPF, Kurt: *Gustav Mahler* (Trans. Inge Goodwin; London 1973)
*Mahler – A Documentary Biography* (Thames & Hudson, London)

CARDUS, Neville: *Gustav Mahler. The Man and his Music* (Vol. 1; Gollancz, London 1965)

COOKE, Deryck: *Gustav Mahler. An Introduction to his Music* (Ed. Colin Matthews, David Matthews; Faber, 1980)

DE LA GRANGE, Henry-Louis: *Mahler Vol. 1* (Gollancz, London 1976)

DEL-MAR, Norman: *Mahler's Sixth Symphony – a study* (Eulenburg, 1980)

GARTENBERG, Egon: *Mahler. The Man and his Music* (Cassell, London 1978)

KENNEDY, Michael: *Mahler* (Dent Master Musicians Series, London 1974)

MAHLER, Alma Maria: *Gustav Mahler. Memories and Letters* (Trans. Basil Creighton, Ed. with footnotes and intro. by Donald Mitchell; John Murray, London 1968)
*And the Bridge is Love – an autobiography* (Hutchinson, London 1959)
*Selected Letters of Gustav Mahler.* Edited by Knud Martner (Orign. edition selected by Alma Mahler) (Faber, London 1979)

MITCHELL, Donald: *Gustav Mahler. The Early Years* (First Published 1958. Revised with critical appendix by Paul Banks and David Matthews; Faber, London 1958)
*The Wunderhorn Years* (Faber, London 1975)

WALTER, Bruno: *Gustav Mahler* (Revised Ed. and trans. by Lotte Walter Lindt; Hamish Hamilton, London 1958)

WALTER, Bruno: *Theme & Variations – an autobiography* (Trans. James A. Galston; Hamish Hamilton, London 1947)

The above represents a very selective list of suggestions for further reading. I would particularly draw attention to the late Deryck Cooke's perceptive and lucid introduction to the music itself. Since the one sure way towards a complete understanding of Mahler, the man, must be through his music, and since, for the purposes of my book I have avoided detailed analysis of his scores, I really cannot conceive of a more useful companion to the volume which you now have in front of you.

Among other sources – which, I need hardly add, have been multifarious – I gratefully acknowledge the following works from which I have borrowed a number of illuminating passages: both Alma Mahler's fascinating books, noted above, the source of so many revealing letters; Bruno Walter's intimate studies; Max Graf's 'Legend of a Musical City' (The Story of Vienna); Richard Schickel's 'The World of Carnegie Hall'; CBS Records' splendid archival compilation of radio interviews, 'Gustav Mahler remembered', edited by Deryck Cooke and originally issued in conjunction with their Leonard Bernstein recording of the Sixth Symphony; and an excellent article on the background to Mahler's Tenth Symphony by Michael Steinberg (Artistic Adviser of the San Francisco Symphony Orchestra) reprinted in the booklet accompanying EMI's recording of Deryck Cooke's final version.

Edward Seckerson, London 1982

# Index